SHOCKING ELECTRICITY

hinkler

Rob Colson

SAFETY & INSTRUCTIONS FOR PARENTS

A NOTE FOR PARENTS

Do not manipulate the protective devices on the items in this kit or on any of the other required items used within this book. Current-limiting devices, such as the rubber protective coating on a device, is there to protect the user and their space from harm. If such devices are tampered with, potential dangers include short-circuiting the item, overheating electrical cords, battery eruption and excessive heating causing burning.

⚠ **WARNING:** Some activities in this publication require tools or materials that could cause serious injury if swallowed or misused. Some activities may not be suitable for all children. Always supervise children when performing the activities described. The publisher and its respective employees and agents will not accept responsibility for injury or damage occasioned to any person or property as a result of participation in any activity described in this book.

ELECTRICAL SAFETY!

Electricity can be very dangerous. While the projects you'll make and study in this book are harmless, you should never, ever play around electric power outlets as it could harm or even kill you! This includes the power outlets you find in your home and especially any power-company transformers and stations that may be in your street. You should also take care beneath electric power lines and wires and never fly a kite, toy plane or drone near them.

ALL ABOUT BATTERIES

Replace by adults only. Batteries are small and can be ingested. Remove and discard all exhausted batteries and install new batteries with correct polarity. Use only batteries of same or equivalent type. Do not mix old and new batteries or alkaline, standard and rechargeable batteries. Do not short-circuit terminals. Do not attempt to recharge non-rechargeable batteries. Rechargeable batteries must be removed from product before being charged and should only be charged under adult supervision.

Please do not dispose of device or used batteries in the household waste. Disposal can take place at appropriate collection points provided in your state. To reduce the impact on human health and the environment, dispose of items at your retail store or at appropriate collection sites according to national or local regulations.

YOUR TOOLBOX

Here are some tools and utensils you will need (but you may need an adult's assistance!):

- Craft knife
- Hammer
- Pencil sharpener
- Pliers
- Saw
- Scissors
- Sharp knife

Published in 2025 by Curious Universe UK Ltd
UK - The Ice House, 124-126 Walcot Street, Bath BA1 5BG
EU - Münsterstraße 5, 59065 Hamm, Germany
www.curiousuniverse.co.uk

© Hinkler Pty Ltd 2024

Cover design: Sam Grimmer
Images © Hinkler Books Pty Ltd or Shutterstock.com

All rights reserved. No part of this publication may be reproduced, stored in a retrieval system or transmitted in any way or by any means, electronic, mechanical, photocopying, recording or otherwise, without the prior written permission of Hinkler Books Pty Ltd.

ISBN 978 1 4889 6600 2

Printed and bound in China

⚠ **WARNING:**

Never connect the terminals of the battery holder when it contains the batteries. Always remove the batteries from the battery holder when not in use. In case of overheating, disconnect battery leads, remove batteries and allow to cool. Carefully check wiring before reconnecting.

CONTENTS

GET READY FOR ELECTRICITY!   4

CIRCUITS   6

SWITCHES   14

CONDUCTORS AND INSULATORS   22

ELECTROMAGNETS   30

STATIC ELECTRICITY   38

BATTERIES   46

SOLAR POWER   54

SOLAR CAR   62

GET READY FOR ELECTRICITY!

The electricity projects in this book are easy to make and huge fun to play around with. Each chapter starts with an introduction that will tell you all you need to know about the experiments that follow. From just a handful of items, you will build 50 different gadgets – from electromagnets to a burglar alarm and from a car powered by sunlight to an electric train.

LOOK OUT FOR:

ASK AN ADULT!
Some projects involve stages that need to be carried out by an adult, such as using a sharp knife. Wherever you need an adult's help, you will see this symbol:

MESS ALERT!
Be prepared – whenever things get yucky and messy, you will see this symbol:

WHAT'S IN THIS KIT?

Along with this book, you'll find a whole load of equipment to help build your electricity projects. As well as everything you need to make a solar-powered racing car, there are motors, a clock, wires, LED light globes and a buzzer!

SOLAR CAR KIT

Nuts x 10, bolts x 10 and washers x 4

Screwdriver

Brackets

Alligator leads x 4

Buzzer

Light globes x 2 (3V)
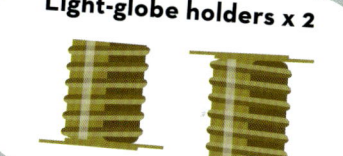

Motor
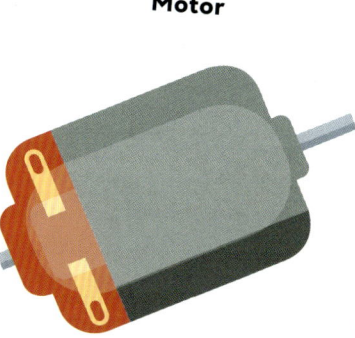

LED light globes x 3
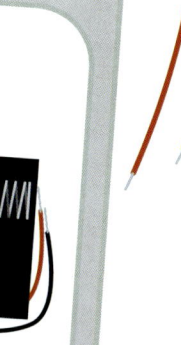

Light-globe holders x 2

LCD clock

Battery holder

SCIENCE KIT

Gear

Solar panel and motor

Chassis

Wheels x 4

Axles x 2
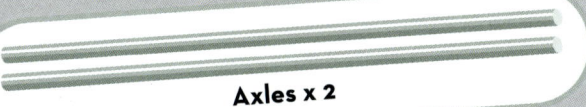

CIRCUITS

From the lights in our homes to the phones in our pockets, electricity powers the modern world. It is produced by the flow of tiny particles called electrons. To start a flow of electrons, you need to make an electric circuit.

SIMPLE CIRCUITS

A simple circuit contains three parts:
1. a power source, such as a cell or battery
2. wires that conduct electricity
3. a component, such as a light globe, which is powered by the electricity.

For the electrons to travel around a circuit, the circuit must be complete. This means that there cannot be any gaps. For example, cutting a wire stops the flow of electrons.

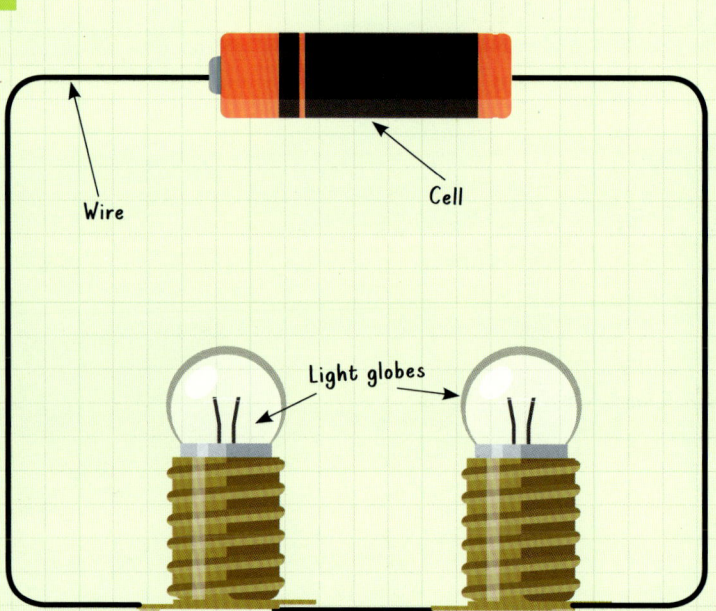

PRO-TIP
For all the experiments, be sure not to let the alligator clips touch one another. Doing this could cause a short-circuit that could damage the batteries.

POSITIVE OR NEGATIVE?

Electrons have a negative electric charge. If you look at a battery, you will see the symbols − and + on each end. When a battery is part of a complete circuit, electrons flow around the circuit from the negative (−) end to the positive end (+). This is called an electric current. Batteries have a voltage marked on them. This is a measure of how hard the battery 'pushes' the current around the circuit. Machinery in homes and factories requires high voltages, while smaller devices such as a wristwatch will run on much lower voltages.

CIRCUITS

Words you need to know

COMPONENTS
Machines or gadgets, such as lights, that are powered by an electric current.

ELECTRIC CHARGE
The amount of electricity held by an object. An object may have a positive charge or a negative charge.

ELECTRON
Electrons are part of atoms, the tiny particles that make up everything. Electrons have a negative electric charge.

TRANSISTOR
A device that alters the flow of electricity. Transistors are used in televisions and radios.

VOLTAGE
An electric pressure produced between two different places. A voltage is needed for electricity to flow through a circuit.

ELECTRIC HEARTBEATS

Did you know that electricity keeps you alive? Not only does electricity run our world, it also runs your body! The muscle cells in our hearts are controlled by electrical signals. We can detect the electricity with a machine called an electrocardiogram (ECG). This machine measures the electricity flowing through a person's heart and displays a line that spikes with every heartbeat.

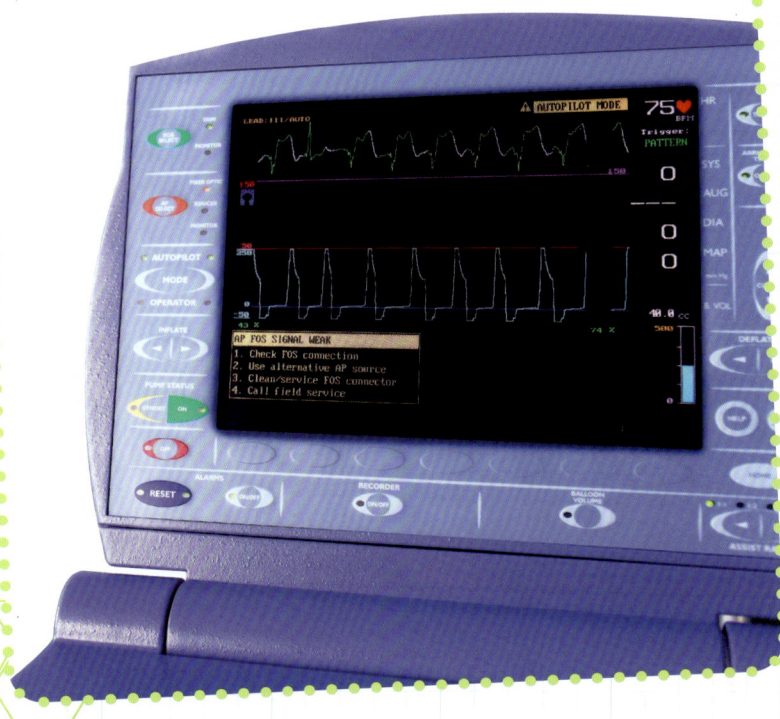

MICRO CIRCUITS

Integrated Circuits (ICs), otherwise known as microchips, are found inside most electronic devices. These are highly complex circuits that are etched into a tiny silicon chip smaller than your fingernail. Each chip contains many microscopic parts called transistors. Since microchips were invented in 1959, technology has advanced at breakneck speed. The number of transistors on a single chip has roughly doubled every two years: from 2,000 in 1970 to more than 2 billion on a fingernail-size chip today. Amazing!

Tiny microchips can sit on a fingertip!

One microchip
from 2018 has as many transistors in it as
1 million
microchips from 1970.

7

CIRCUITS

1 LET THERE BE LIGHT!

See the power of a continuous electrical circuit by making your own simple one. Connect a light to a circuit and turn dark into day. Then see how easy it is to break a circuit.

WHAT YOU NEED

From the kit:
- Battery holder
- Light globe
- Light-globe holder
- 2 alligator clips

From your home:
- 2 AA batteries

1 Insert the batteries into the battery holder, making sure to line up the batteries in the way shown on the holder. Screw the light globe into its holder.

CURIOUS CURIOSITY

The longest electric circuit in the world is the SEA-ME-WE 3 communications cable. It extends from Australia to Western Europe, linking up 33 different countries along the way. The circuit is a staggering 39,000 kilometres (24,000 miles) long – nearly long enough to go around the entire planet.

2 Connect the teeth of alligator clip 1 to one of the wires attached to the battery holder. Connect the teeth of alligator clip 2 to the other wire attached to the battery holder.

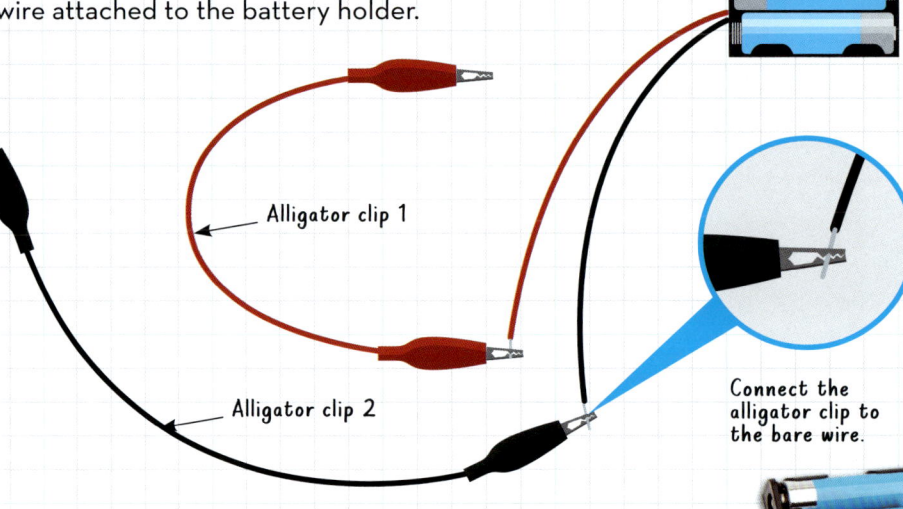

Connect the alligator clip to the bare wire.

What's the SCIENCE?

Connecting the globe to both ends of the battery completes a continuous circuit for the electricity to flow. The globe glows because it resists the flow a little, turning the energy in the electricity into light energy. The greater a bulb's resistance, the brighter it will shine.

3 Connect the other end of each alligator clip to each side of the globe holder. You should now have a closed circle between the batteries and globe. This completes the circuit, making the light globe glow! If you disconnect either of the alligator clips, the circuit breaks and the light globe goes out.

Alligator clips connect to either side of the globe holder

Alligator clip connected to globe holder and battery wire

CIRCUITS

LINE OF LIGHTS 2

You can wire up lights in different ways. Light up two bulbs at once by creating a series circuit. But be careful – when one goes out, they all go out!

WHAT YOU NEED
From the kit:
- Battery holder
- 2 light globes
- 2 light-globe holders
- 3 alligator clips

From your home:
- 2 AA batteries

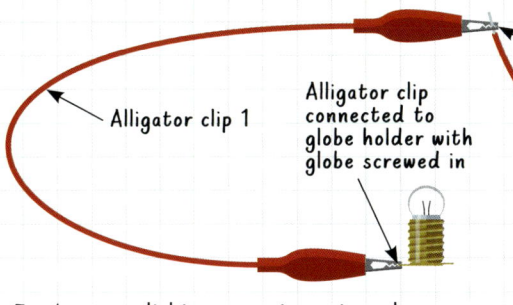

1. As you did in experiment 1, place the batteries into the battery holder and screw the light globes into their holders.

2. Connect one wire of the battery holder to the first globe holder using alligator clip 1.

3. Use alligator clip 2 to connect the second globe holder to the first globe holder.

4. Connect one end of alligator clip 3 to the second globe and the other end of the alligator clip to the other wire on the battery holder, closing the circuit. The globes should both light up! How bright are the light globes? Are they brighter or dimmer than the single globe circuit?

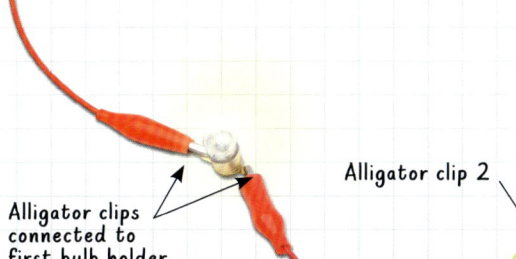

What's the SCIENCE?

This way of connecting the globes is called a series circuit. When the globes are connected in a series, the flow of electricity passes from the battery to the first globe, then to the second and back to the other end of the battery. If you disconnect any of the globes, they will all go out because you have broken the circuit. Each light globe uses half the voltage, so they are dimmer than one on its own.

... TAKE IT FURTHER!
Try disconnecting one of the wires from one of the light globes and see for yourself!

 **CURIOUS CURIOSITY**
Christmas-tree lights are often connected in a series. If they all go out, you have to check every bulb in turn to find the one that has broken. Once the broken bulb has been replaced, all the lights should work again.

9

CIRCUITS

3 PARALLEL LIGHTS

Now try another way of wiring up bulbs by creating a parallel circuit. With this type of circuit, when one globe goes out, the other will stay on.

WHAT YOU NEED

From the kit:
- Battery holder
- 2 light globes
- 2 light-globe holders
- 4 alligator clips

From your home:
- 2 AA batteries

1 Connect up one light globe to the battery to form a continuous circuit, as on page 10.

- Alligator clip 1
- Alligator clip connected to bare wire
- Batteries placed in battery holder
- Alligator clip connected to bare wire
- Alligator clip 2
- Screw light globe into holder
- Alligator clips connected to first globe holder

2 Connect the second globe by attaching alligator clips 3 and 4 to either side of the second globe holder. Then attach the other ends of clips 3 and 4 to the clips connected to the first globe holder.

- Alligator clip 1
- Alligator clip 2
- Alligator clip 3
- Alligator clip 4
- Alligator clip connected to globe holder

3 Now disconnect either alligator clip 3 or 4. The first light globe should stay on, but how bright is it now?

CURIOUS CURIOSITY

The electrical outlets in your home are connected to the national power supply along parallel circuits. This allows you to use just the outlets that you need. If they were connected in series, all devices and plugged-in gadgets in your home would need to be turned on all the time!

What's the SCIENCE?

In this parallel circuit, the current from the battery is divided up into two streams. Each stream goes through just one light globe, meaning that each light globe receives the full voltage of the battery. Because of this, light globes in parallel shine more brightly than those in series.

GETTING THE POINT 4

CIRCUITS

Lots of surprising things around the home can carry an electric current. Don't believe us? See what happens when you add a pencil to your circuit.

WHAT YOU NEED

From the kit:
- Battery holder
- Light globe
- Light-globe holder
- 3 alligator clips

From your home:
- 2 AA batteries
- Graphite pencil
- Pencil sharpener

1 Sharpen your pencil so that it is pointed at both ends.

2 Use alligator clip 1 to connect one wire from the battery holder to the light globe in its holder.

3 Attach alligator clip 2 to the other side of the light globe.

4 Connect alligator clip 3 to the other wire of the battery holder. This should leave one end of alligator clip 2 and one end of alligator clip 3 free.

5 Take the two free ends of the alligator clips and connect them to one another. This will complete the circuit and the light globe will light up.

6 Disconnect these ends of alligator clips 2 and 3 and connect them to the sharpened ends of the pencil. Be sure that they connect to the core of the pencil, not the wood. The light globe should light up again, but more dimly.

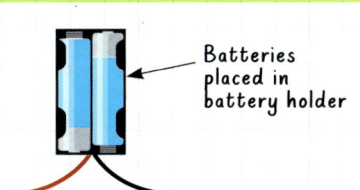

CURIOUS CURIOSITY

Graphite is made from carbon – the same element that diamonds are made from. The atoms in graphite are arranged in layers that slip along each other, which makes graphite soft and easy to write with. The electrons in graphite move easily, allowing it to conduct electricity. Unlike graphite, the carbon atoms in diamonds are arranged in very strong pyramid shapes. Diamond is the hardest natural mineral of all and does not conduct electricity.

What's the SCIENCE?

The core of a pencil is made from a material called graphite. Like metals, graphite can conduct electricity. The graphite allows electricity to pass through it, but it resists some of the flow, making the light glow more dimly.

11

CIRCUITS

5 KITCHEN FOIL CIRCUIT

Have a look through your kitchen cabinets for some aluminium foil and see how this everyday material can be used to make a circuit in place of wires.

WHAT YOU NEED

From the kit:
- Battery holder
- 2 light globes
- 2 light-globe holders

From your home:
- 2 AA batteries
- Aluminium foil
- Roll of tape
- Sheets of paper
- Scissors

1. Ask an adult to cut two long thin strips of foil about 1 cm (½ in) wide. Create bends by folding the foil over to make two strips shaped as shown. Tape the foil strips to a sheet of paper.

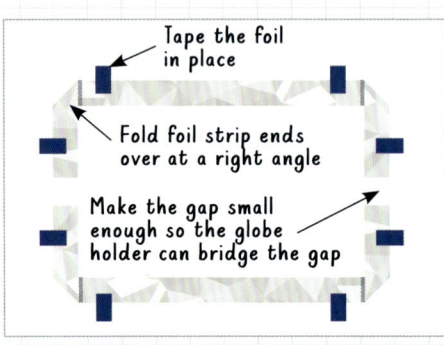

- Tape the foil in place
- Fold foil strip ends over at a right angle
- Make the gap small enough so the globe holder can bridge the gap

CURIOUS CURIOSITY

Never put aluminium foil or any other metal in a microwave oven. If you did, the microwaves would cause electricity to flow and sparks to fly! Microwaves also bounce off the surface of the foil – and away from the food being heated. The window at the front of the oven is coated in a layer of metal mesh. The holes allow us to see inside the oven, but are too small for the microwaves to pass through.

2. Insert your batteries into the battery holder and tape the two wires of the battery holder to the foil at the places marked.

- Batteries placed in battery holder
- Make sure the bare wires are in contact with the foil

3. Screw one of the light globes into the holder and touch the ends of the holder to the foil at the other side to complete the circuit.

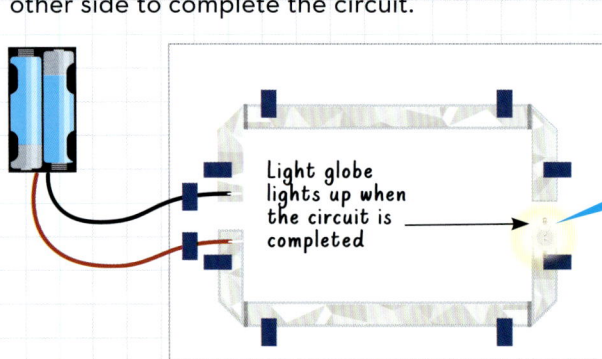
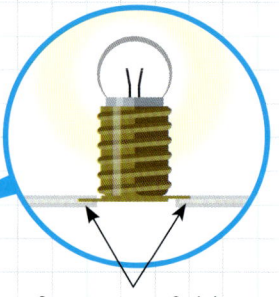

- Light globe lights up when the circuit is completed
- Connections of globe holder should touch ends of foil strips

What's the SCIENCE?

Aluminium is a very good conductor of electricity and is often used to make electric wires. You can make circuits of any shape you like with the flexible foil.

4. Create a parallel circuit for two bulbs by arranging strips of foil in the shape shown here. Both bulbs will light up.

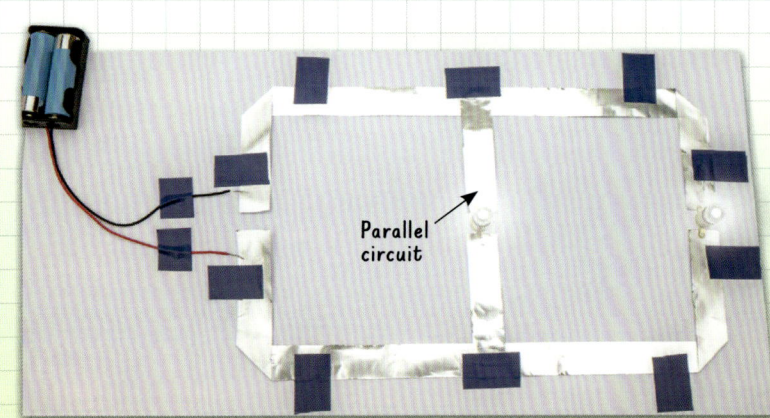

- Parallel circuit

CIRCUITS

SIMPLEST CIRCUIT 6

WHAT YOU NEED
From the kit:
- Battery holder
- Light globe
- Light-globe holder

From your home:
- 2 AA batteries

Connecting your bulb directly to the battery holder is the simplest way to create a circuit.

1 Screw the light globe into the holder and insert your batteries into the battery holder. Connect the wires of the battery holder to both sides of the bulb holder.

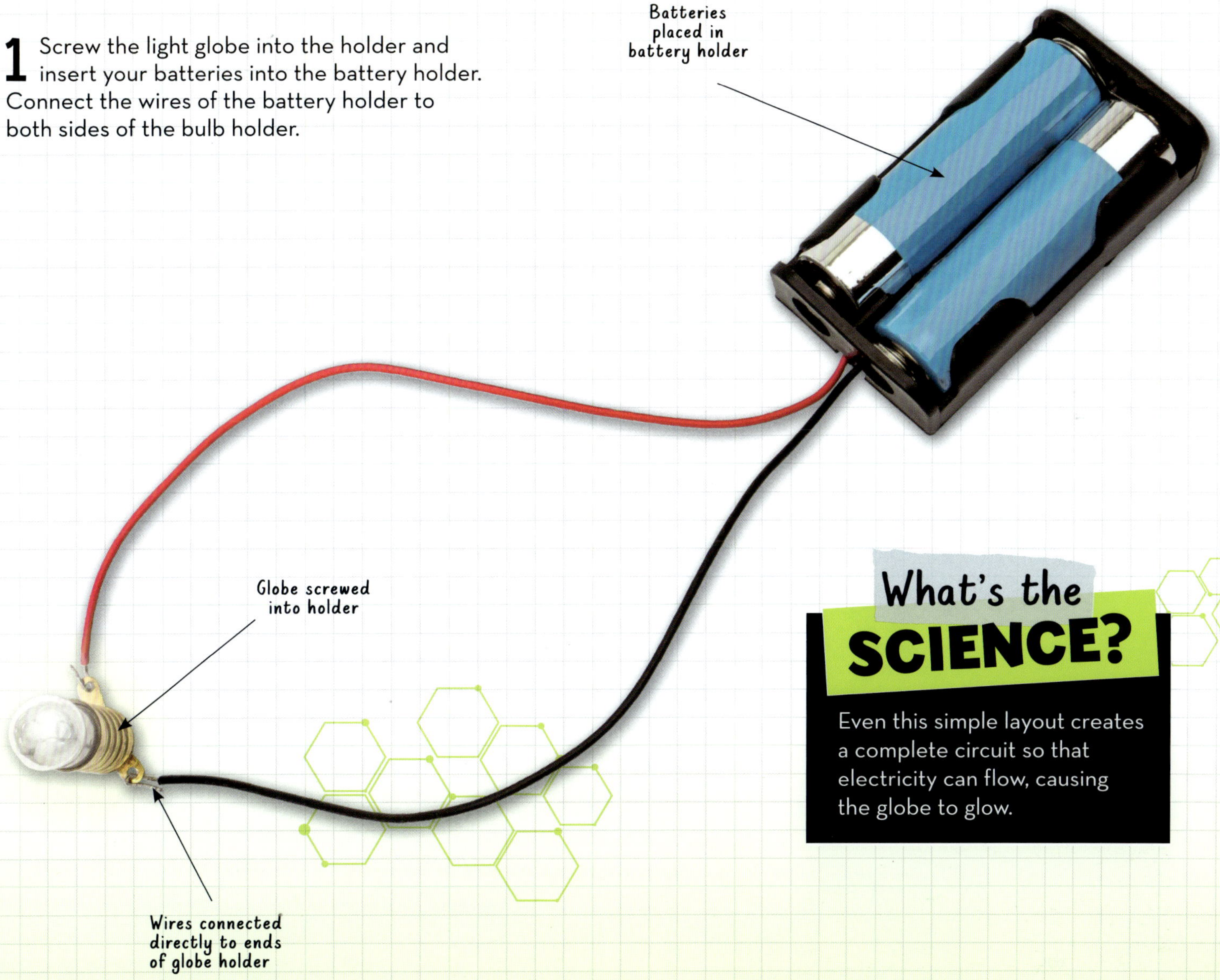

Batteries placed in battery holder

Globe screwed into holder

Wires connected directly to ends of globe holder

What's the SCIENCE?

Even this simple layout creates a complete circuit so that electricity can flow, causing the globe to glow.

13

SWITCHES

Flick a switch and a light comes on. Push a button and the TV powers up. We use switches to control lots of different electrical devices, from small smartphones up to enormous factory machines.

ON AND OFF

A switch consists of a movable part that is used to connect and disconnect an electrical circuit. When the switch is closed, it completes the circuit to allow the flow of electricity. When the switch is open, it breaks the circuit, stopping the flow of electricity and turning the power off.

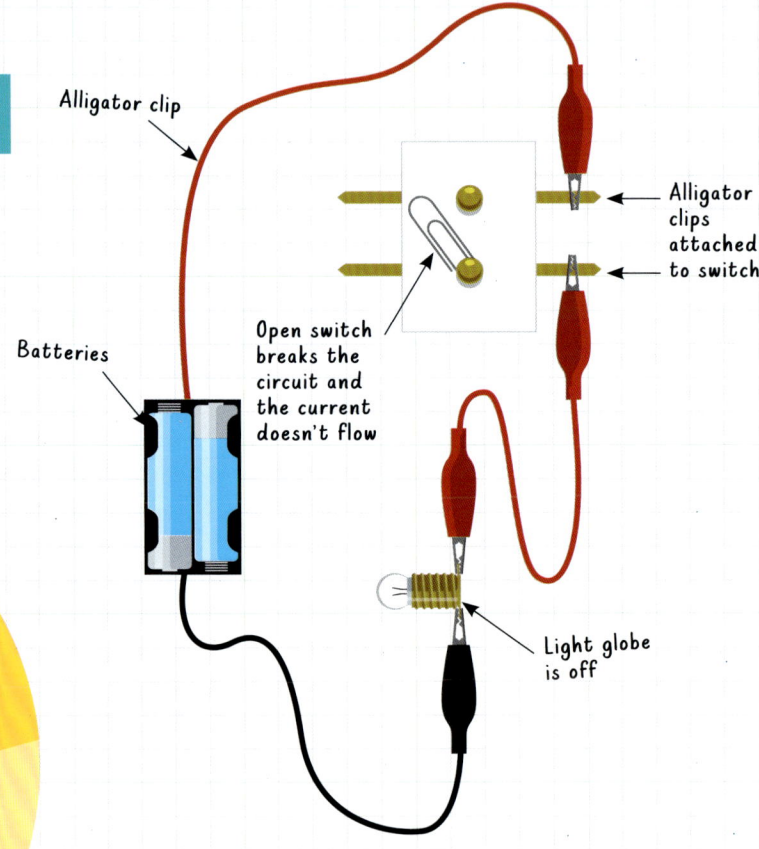

20%

Dimming the lights can reduce electricity usage by

20 PERCENT.

DIMMER SWITCHES

Lots of homes and businesses use dimmer lights so that you can adjust the amount of light in a room. These switches reduce the flow of electricity to dim the lights. One way to do this is to pass the current through a substance that resists the flow, called a resistor. However, this wastes energy by turning some of it into useless heat. Modern dimmer switches overcome this problem in a clever way, by rapidly turning the current on and off to reduce the overall flow. This means that they do not produce wasted heat.

SWITCHES

Words you need to know

FUSE
A device within electric appliances or in the mains electricity supply, which breaks the current if there is an increase in power.

POLARITY
Having two terminals with opposite charge: one negative and one positive.

RESISTOR
A device that makes it more difficult for current to flow around a circuit.

PRO-TIP
The LED globes in your kit have a particular polarity and have to be connected in a particular order. If your LED isn't working, try switching its wires around.

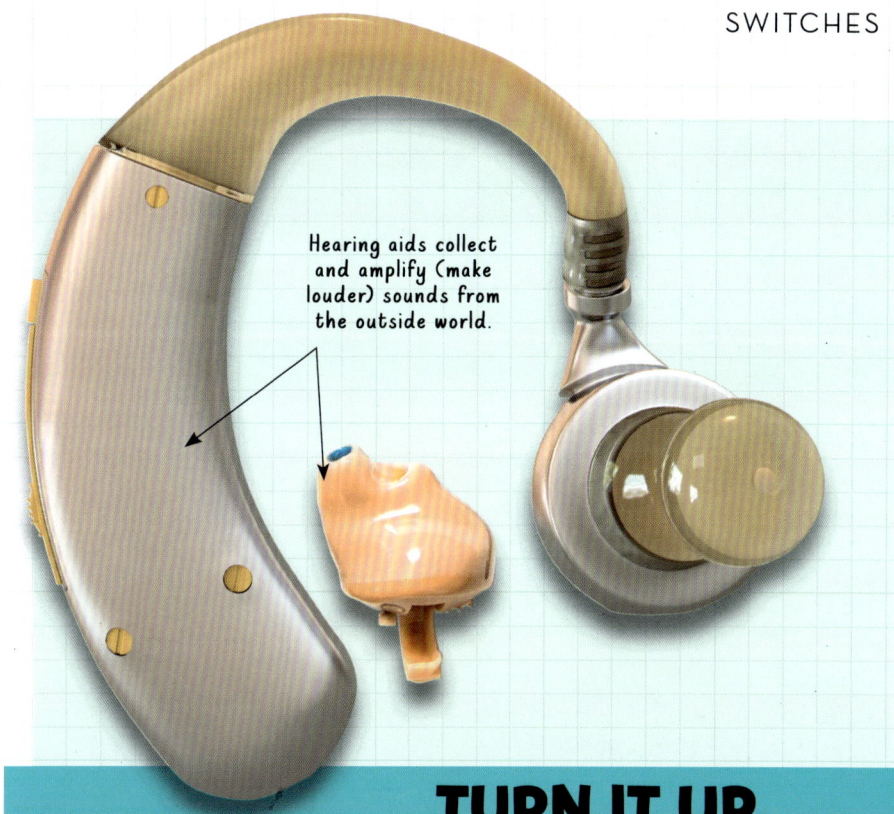

Hearing aids collect and amplify (make louder) sounds from the outside world.

TURN IT UP

The millions of tiny transistors in a microchip can act as both switches and as amplifiers. Amplifiers take in a tiny electric current at one end and produce a much bigger one at the other. For example, hearing aids contain a tiny microphone, which picks up sounds and turns them into an electric current. Transistors use the power from the hearing aid's battery to amplify the current. The larger current powers a tiny speaker, which sends much louder sounds into the ear to help people hear more clearly.

BLOWING A FUSE

Electrical appliances can be damaged by an increase in the strength of the current, which may be caused by faulty wiring or a nearby lightning strike. When you plug in an electric device, it is protected by a fuse, which breaks the circuit if the flow of electricity is too strong. Inside the fuse is a thin piece of wire, which melts when the current passes a particular strength.

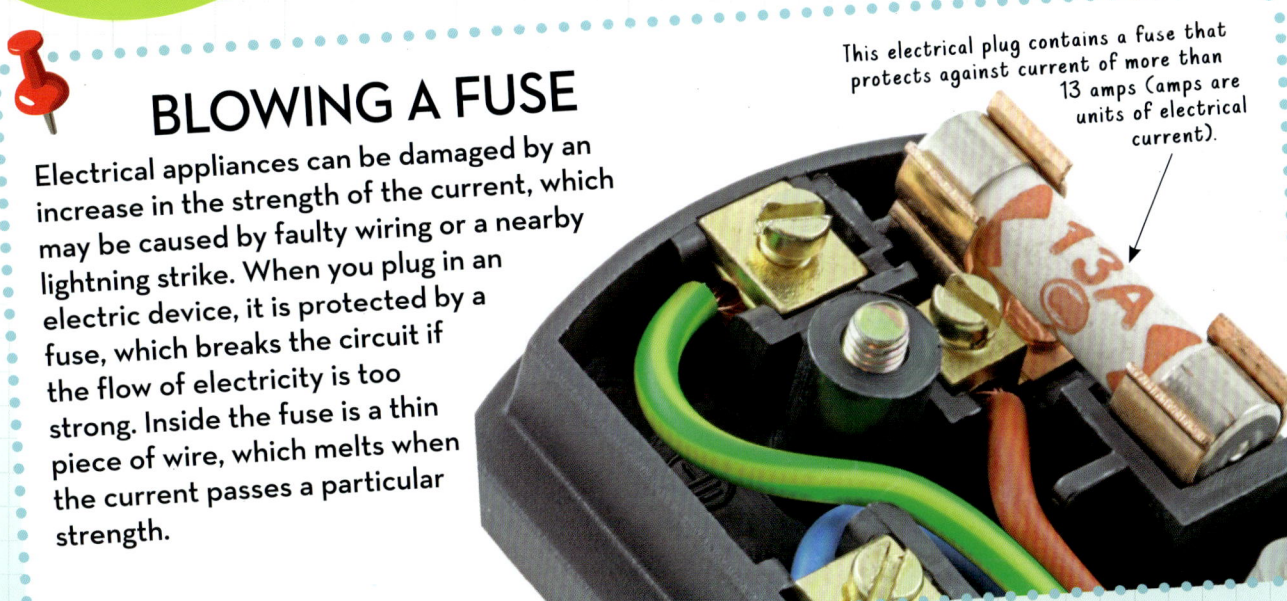

This electrical plug contains a fuse that protects against current of more than 13 amps (amps are units of electrical current).

15

SWITCHES

7 SWITCHING SIDES

Add a switch to your circuit using a paperclip and split pins to give you complete control over the power of electricity.

WHAT YOU NEED

From the kit:
- Battery holder
- Light globe
- Light-globe holder
- 3 alligator clips

From your home:
- 2 split pins
- 2 AA batteries
- Piece of card about 6 x 4 cm (2.3 x 1.6 in)
- Metal paperclip

1 Ask an adult to cut out a rectangular piece of card measuring about 6 x 4 cm (2.3 x 1.6 in). Push the split pins through the card about 2.5 cm (1 in) apart. Flatten them on the other side of the card, making sure that they do not touch one another.

Flatten the arms of the split pins so they sit parallel to each other

Make sure the paperclip is big enough to touch both split pins

2 Turn the card over and push one end of the paperclip under one of the split pins. Rotate so that it does not touch the other pin.

3 Attach alligator clip 1 to one wire of the battery holder and one side of the globe holder. Attach alligator clip 2 to the other end of the globe holder and one of the arms of one of the split pins.

4 Attach alligator clip 3 to the other battery holder wire and an arm from the other split pin. Rotate the paperclip so that it touches both pins and see what happens to the light globe.

CURIOUS CURIOSITY

American inventor Thomas Edison (1847–1934) is credited with more than 2,000 inventions. These include the light bulb, as well as sockets, switches and fuses. In fact, Edison played a part in developing almost everything we need to have electricity delivered to our homes!

What's the SCIENCE?

Touching the paperclip to both split pins at the same time completes the circuit and switches the light globe on. Sliding the paperclip away from one of the split pins breaks the circuit and the light goes off. To give an even light, the paperclip needs to be in firm contact with both pins. Electrical appliances often become faulty because connections have come loose.

Batteries placed in battery holder

Alligator clip 3

Alligator clips attached to the arms of the split pins

Alligator clip 1

Alligator clips connected to the globe holder

Alligator clip 2

16

SWITCHES

BURGLAR ALARM 8

Stop someone sneaking up on you and giving you a nasty shock by making your own pressure alarm.

WHAT YOU NEED

From the kit:
- Battery holder
- 3 alligator clips
- Buzzer

From your home:
- 2 AA batteries
- Roll of aluminium foil
- 3 sheets of cardboard cut to 30 x 30 cm (12 x 12 in)
- Tape or glue stick
- Small plate
- Scissors

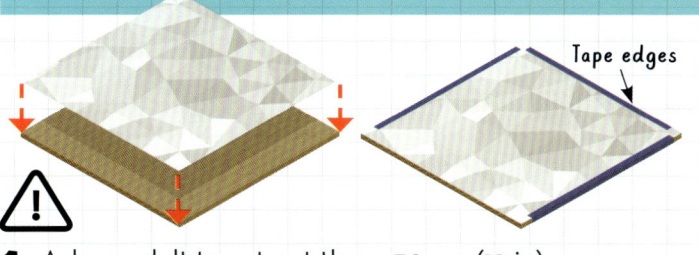

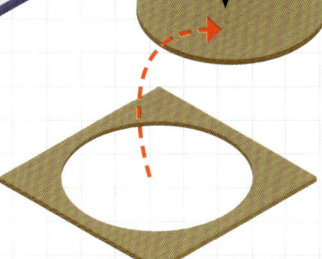

1 Ask an adult to cut out three 30-cm (12-in) squares of cardboard and tape aluminium foil to one side of two of the sheets of cardboard. Draw a circle on the other square using the plate as a template and cut the circle out.

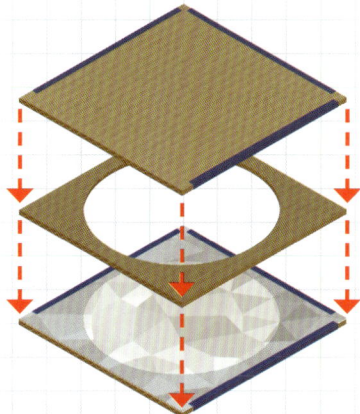

2 Place one square with aluminium face-up at the bottom, the square with the hole in the middle and the third square with aluminium face-down at the top. Tape them together.

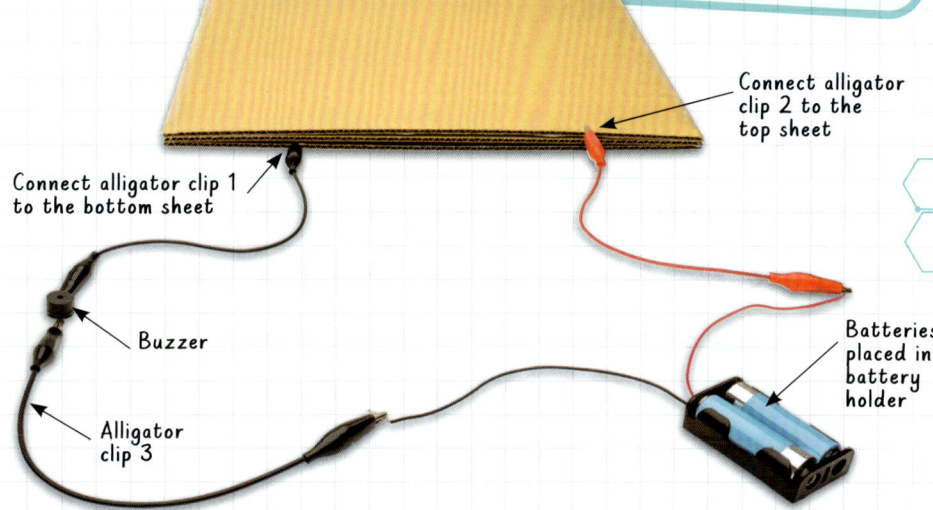

3 Clip alligator clip 1 to the bottom cardboard square (making sure it's in contact with the foil) and to one leg of the buzzer. Connect alligator clip 2 to the top cardboard square and to one lead from the battery holder.

4 Connect alligator clip 3 to the other lead of the battery holder and the other leg of the buzzer. Now squeeze your alarm by pressing on the cardboard. Does the buzzer sound?

CURIOUS CURIOSITY

Fort Knox in Kentucky protects the United States' gold reserve, which is estimated to be worth US$270 billion. The gold is protected by alarms, electric fences and 30,000 troops!

What's the SCIENCE?

When someone treads on the cardboard, they press the aluminium sheets together to complete the circuit, causing the alarm to buzz.

SWITCHES

9 BEAT THE BUZZER

Challenge your friends to this wire maze game! Complete the maze without touching the wire to beat the buzzer. You will need steady hands!

1 To make your wire maze, bend one length of poseable wire into your challenging maze shape. Push both ends into the foam sheet so the wire maze stands upright.

2 With your second piece of poseable wire, make a small hoop so that it goes around the first length of wire. Wrap electrical tape around the other end of the second wire to make a handle, but leaving the tip bare.

3 Connect alligator clip 1 to the bare tip of the handle and one of the leads from the battery holder.

4 Connect alligator clip 2 to the other battery holder lead and one leg of the buzzer. Connect alligator clip 3 to the other buzzer leg and the other end of the wire maze. Wrap modelling clay around both ends of the maze.

5 Guide your wire hoop around the maze without touching the sides. Can you do it? Touch the maze and the buzzer will go off. You lose!

WHAT YOU NEED

From the kit:
- Battery holder
- 3 alligator clips
- Buzzer

From your home:
- 2 AA batteries
- 2 x 60-cm (24-in) lengths of poseable wire (modelling wire)
- Foam sheet – 30 x 30 cm (12 x 12 in) square
- Electrical tape
- Modelling clay

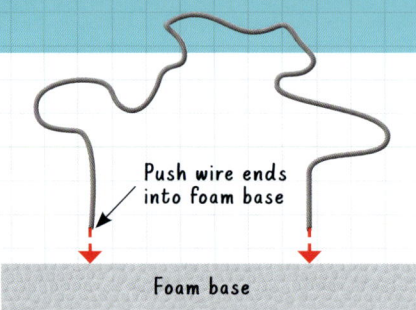
Push wire ends into foam base
Foam base

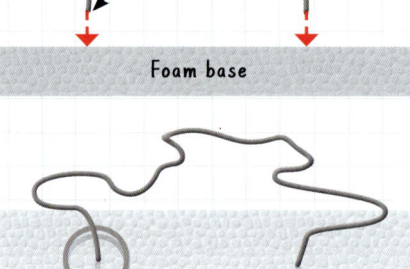

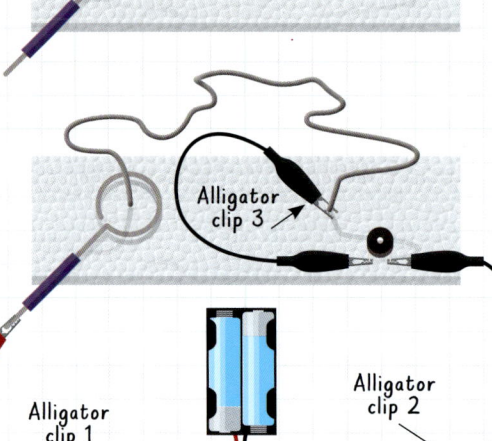
Alligator clip 3
Alligator clip 1
Alligator clip 2

CURIOUS CURIOSITY

A steady hand is an essential requirement for a bomb-disposal expert. As with your electric wire maze, a bomb-disposal expert needs to be careful what they touch to disconnect the wiring of the bomb; the slightest twitch could cause an explosion. That's the ultimate test of calm under pressure!

What's the SCIENCE?

When the wire hoop touches the wire maze, it completes the circuit, sounding the buzzer.

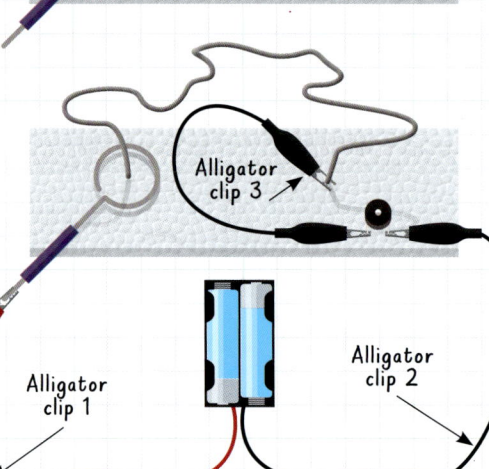

SWITCHES

DIM THE LIGHTS 10

Are your lights too bright? Make a switch out of a pencil core and dim their brightness as you slide the switch.

1 Attach alligator clip 1 to one end of the pencil core and to one wire from the battery holder.

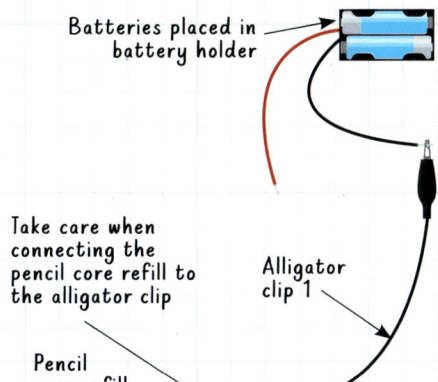

Batteries placed in battery holder

Take care when connecting the pencil core refill to the alligator clip

Alligator clip 1

Pencil core refill

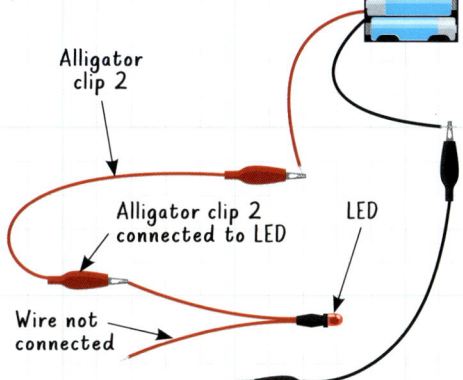

Alligator clip 2

Alligator clip 2 connected to LED

LED

Wire not connected

WHAT YOU NEED

From the kit:
- Battery holder
- 2 alligator clips
- LED light

From your home:
- 2 AA batteries
- Pencil core refills

2 Connect alligator clip 2 to the other wire from the battery holder and to one wire from the LED light.

CURIOUS CURIOSITY

The first dimmer switches were made for theaters. The current was controlled by passing it through variable depths of salt water, which was stored in large cylinders. The switches were dangerous to use and would often make the operator's hairs stand on end!

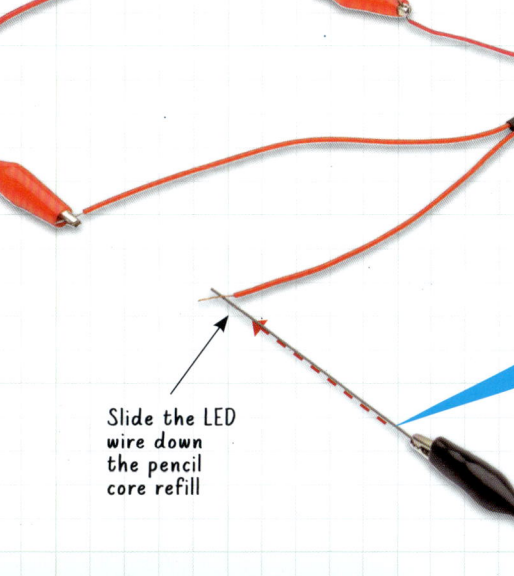

Slide the LED wire down the pencil core refill

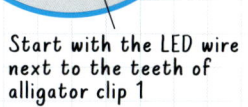

Start with the LED wire next to the teeth of alligator clip 1

What's the SCIENCE?

The circuit is completed by passing the current through the pencil core, which is made from graphite. The further you move the alligator clip away from the wire, the longer the length of graphite that the current must pass through. This creates more resistance, reducing the current and dimming the light.

3 Touch the bare wire of the LED to the pencil core in the alligator clip. Keeping contact with the core, slide the wire down the core. Does the LED become dimmer?

SWITCHES

11 READY, STEADY, GO!

Create a set of traffic lights and switch from one light to the next with a popsicle-stick switch.

WHAT YOU NEED

From the kit:
- Battery holder
- Red, yellow and green LED lights
- 2 alligator clips

From your home:
- Craft stick
- 2 AA batteries
- Cardboard tube, about 5 cm (2 in) in diameter
- Foam sheet – 30 x 30 cm (12 x 12 in)
- Tape
- Aluminium foil
- 3 drawing pins

1 Ask an adult to pierce three small holes in one side of the cardboard tube and cut out a small tab at the bottom on the reverse side, as shown.

Front with holes made

Back with slot cut out

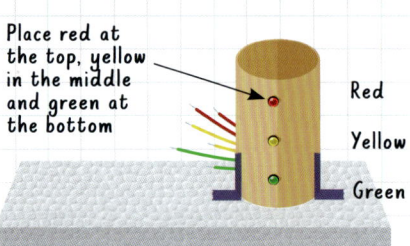
Place red at the top, yellow in the middle and green at the bottom

2 Feed the wires from the LEDs through the holes and tape the tube to the foam sheet.

3 Twist the shorter wire from each of the LEDs together and connect them to the negative terminal of the battery holder with alligator clip 1.

4 Push the drawing pins into the foam sheet in a line. Wrap the bare ends of the free wires from each of the LEDs to each pin, with the yellow LED in the centre.

CURIOUS CURIOSITY

The first traffic lights were installed outside the Houses of Parliament in London, England, in 1868. There were just two lights: red for stop and green for go. However, the lights exploded after a few weeks and had to be taken down.

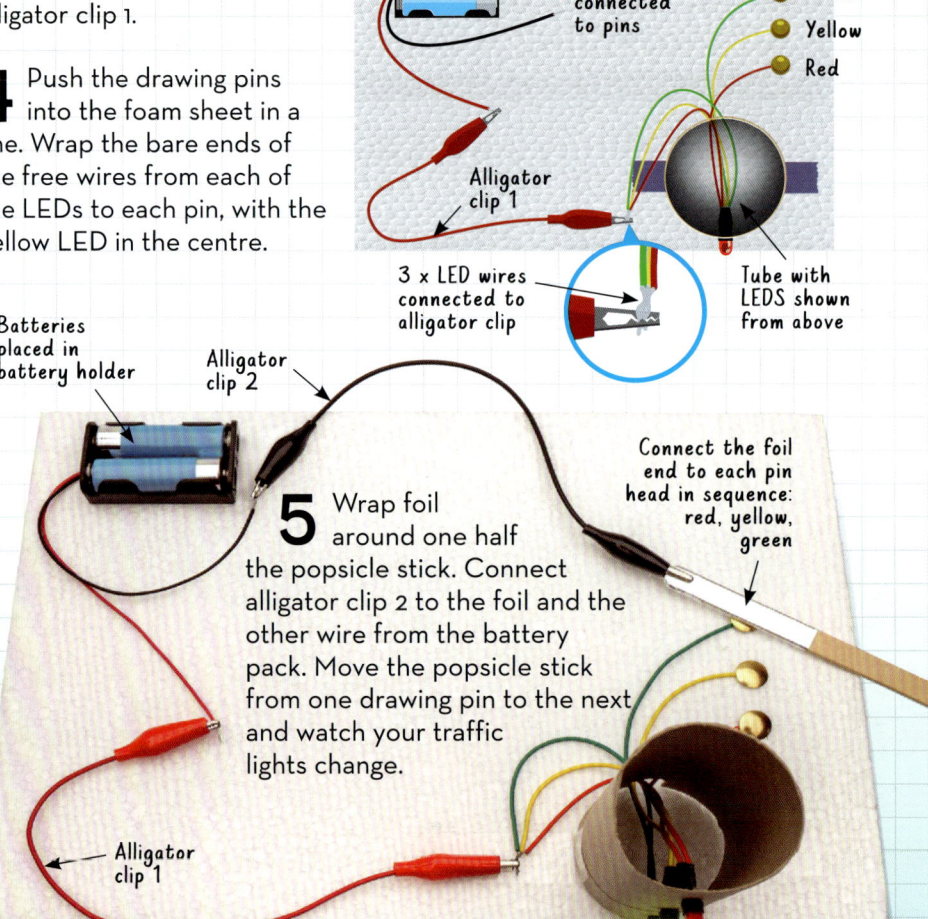

5 Wrap foil around one half the popsicle stick. Connect alligator clip 2 to the foil and the other wire from the battery pack. Move the popsicle stick from one drawing pin to the next and watch your traffic lights change.

What's the SCIENCE?

You have turned the popsicle stick into a switch! The current flows through the aluminium foil and the drawing pin to complete the circuit through one of the three LEDs.

SWITCHES

DOUBLE SWITCH 12

WHAT YOU NEED
From the kit:
- Battery holder
- 4 alligator clips
- Light globe
- Light-globe holder

From your home:
- 4 split pins
- 2 AA batteries
- Small sheet of cardboard
- 2 paperclips

Build a double switch and turn your lights on and off from different locations.

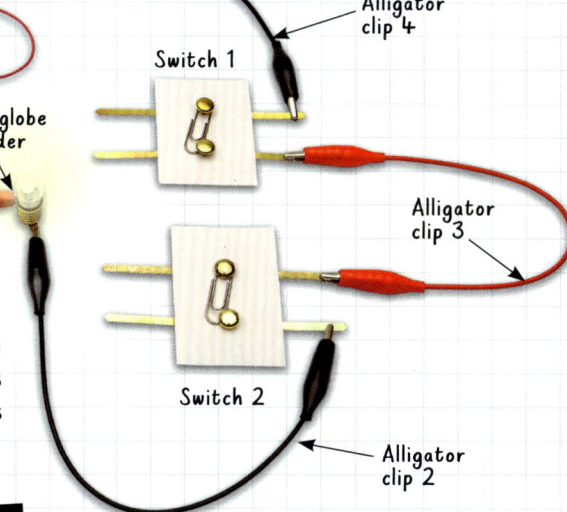

1. Follow the instructions on page 18 to make two switches using the split pins. Connect them to the battery holder and globe as shown here. Operate the switches to turn the globe on and off.

What's the SCIENCE?

Both switches need to be on to complete the circuit and turn the globe on. But you can break the circuit from either switch to turn the globe off.

13 ROLL THE BALL

Make a switch that is operated by rolling a marble.

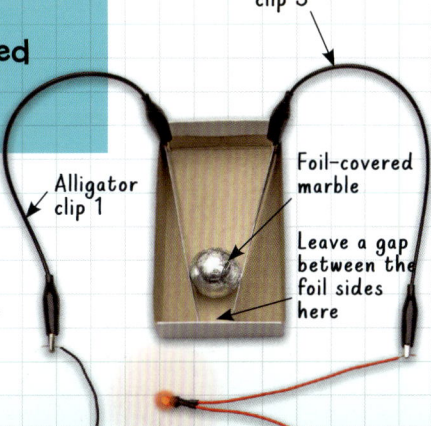

1. Fold two pieces of foil and tape them inside the drawer of the matchbox to form a 'V'. Leave a gap in the middle at the narrow end of the 'V'. Attach alligator clip 1 to one foil strip and the negative wire from the battery holder. Attach alligator clip 2 to the positive wire from the battery holder wire and the longer wire from the LED.

2. Attach alligator clip 3 to the shorter LED wire and the other foil strip. Wrap foil around the marble and put it at the other end of the matchbox. Roll the marble down the matchbox to light up the LED.

WHAT YOU NEED
From the kit:
- Battery holder
- 3 alligator clips
- LED light

From your home:
- 2 AA batteries
- Small glass marble
- Aluminium foil
- Matchbox
- Tape

What's the SCIENCE?

The aluminium wrapped around the marble completes the circuit as long as it is in contact with both strips of aluminium foil.

21

CONDUCTORS AND INSULATORS

CONDUCTORS AND INSULATORS

Electricity travels very easily through some materials. These are known as conductors. Other materials don't allow electricity to pass through them. These are known as insulators.

CONDUCTORS

The wires in an electric circuit are made out of metal. Metals, such as iron and copper and graphite (a form of carbon), found in the core of pencils, are the only solids that conduct electricity well. They do so because they contain electrons that can move freely.

INSULATORS

If you handle the cord from an electrical gadget, you won't get a shock because the protective coating around an electric wire is made out of plastic. Plastic is a good insulator and it is very flexible. All of the electrons in plastic are bound to their atoms and they cannot easily move. Before plastic, rubber was used to insulate wires. Rubber is also a good insulator, but over time it would harden and crack, making the wires dangerous.

Wire

Plastic

SEMICONDUCTOR

Silicon, a common element found in sand, is a material that falls between conductors and insulators, known as a semiconductor. Its ability to conduct electricity is increased by adding impurities, such as substances like phosphorus or boron. Microchips are created by baking patterns of impurities across the silicon. These allow electricity to pass along certain pathways but not others, creating complex circuits.

The microchips in computers and smartphones are made from silicon.

CONDUCTORS AND INSULATORS

Words you need to know

CONDUCTOR
A substance that easily allows an electric current to flow through it.

INSULATOR
A substance that does not allow an electric current to flow through it.

IONS
These are atoms that have become electrically charged and can have either a positive or a negative charge.

SEMICONDUCTOR
A substance that conducts electricity at varying amounts depending on its purity and temperature.

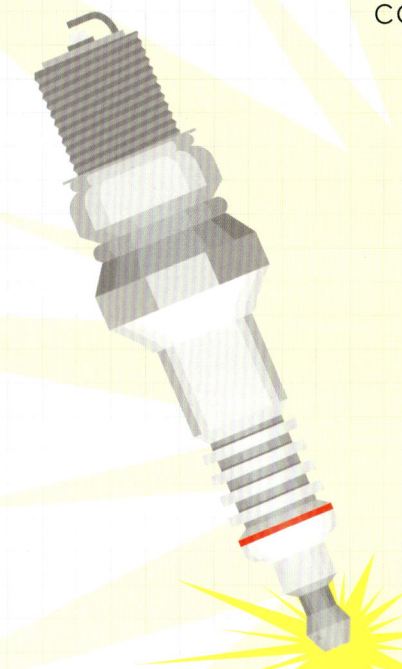

SPARKS FLYING
At low voltages, air does not conduct electricity. However, with a high-enough voltage, charged particles called ions are created in the air and an electric current can pass through it as a spark. For example, spark plugs create sparks in the air to ignite the fuel in a car engine.

WATER DANGER!
Pure water is a very good insulator, so how can water be dangerous? The secret is found in the minerals that some water can contain. The minerals dissolve to create charged particles in the water that can move freely, carrying electric current and turning water into a conductor.

Electric eels stun their prey by sending out powerful electric currents through the water.

PRO-TIP
Even the best conductors offer a little resistance (unless they're superconductors!). If you find that some of your kit starts to get a bit warm, disconnect the batteries and leave things to cool down.

SUPERCONDUCTORS
Even good conductors of electricity, such as copper or aluminium, resist the flow of electrons a little. But some materials lose all resistance at ultra-low temperatures. In these materials, known as superconductors, a current can continue to flow without ever getting weaker.

CONDUCTORS AND INSULATORS

14 MODELLING CLAY CIRCUIT

Even a child's toy can be used to carry electricity! See how you can complete a circuit using modelling clay.

WHAT YOU NEED
From the kit:
- Battery holder
- LED light

From your home:
- 2 AA batteries
- To make your modelling clay, you need 2 bowls, plain flour, salt, vegetable oil and food colouring

1. To make your own modelling clay, follow this recipe: In a large bowl, mix 8 tablespoons of plain flour with 2 tablespoons of salt. In a separate bowl, mix 60 ml (2 fl oz) of warm water, a few drops of food colouring in your favourite colour and 1 tablespoon of vegetable oil. Pour the contents of the second bowl into the large bowl and mix. Knead the mixture with your hands for a few minutes to form a smooth, flexible 'clay'.

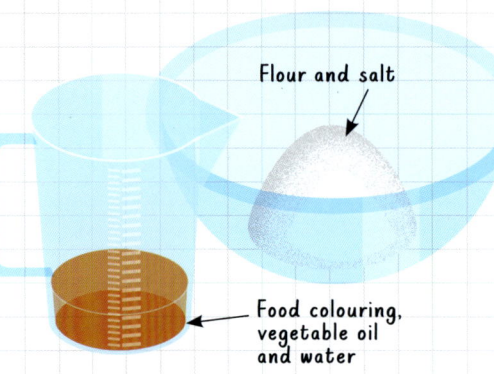

2. Create two thin 'sausages' of modelling clay and insert one connection from the battery holder into one end of each 'sausage'.

CURIOUS CURIOSITY
Play-Doh™ was invented in the late 1940s by Noah McVicker. He originally created it as a putty to clean wallpaper. Local school teacher Kay Zufall used the putty in art projects in class. It proved such a hit that she persuaded McVicker to start selling his putty to children.

What's the SCIENCE?

Modelling clay conducts electricity because it contains salty water. It also resists the flow of electricity a little, so the further the current has to travel through the modelling clay, the dimmer the LED will glow.

... TAKE IT FURTHER!
Try inserting the LED wires at different points along the 'sausages'. Does the globe get dimmer or brighter?

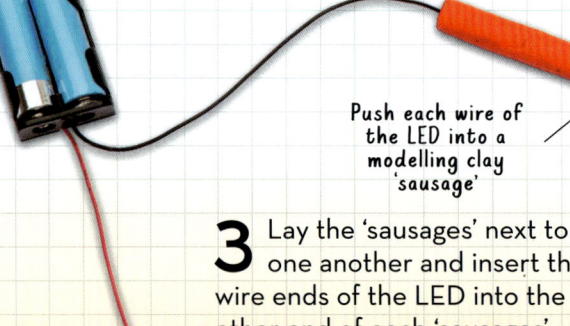

3. Lay the 'sausages' next to one another and insert the wire ends of the LED into the other end of each 'sausages'. Does your LED light up?

24

CONDUCTORS AND INSULATORS

DRAW YOUR OWN CIRCUIT 15

No wires handy to complete a circuit? You can draw your own working circuit on a piece of card with a pencil!

WHAT YOU NEED

From the kit:
- 2 alligator clips
- LED light

From your home:
- 9V battery
- HB or softer pencil
- Small piece of card
- Tape

1 Draw out a thick line with your pencil onto the piece of card. Draw from the edge of the card to a place near the middle.

Make your pencil line nice and thick

Try using as soft a pencil as possible, such as a 4–6B

2 Connect alligator clip 1 to the positive terminal on the battery and to the end of the thick pencil line. Connect alligator clip 2 to the negative terminal on the battery.

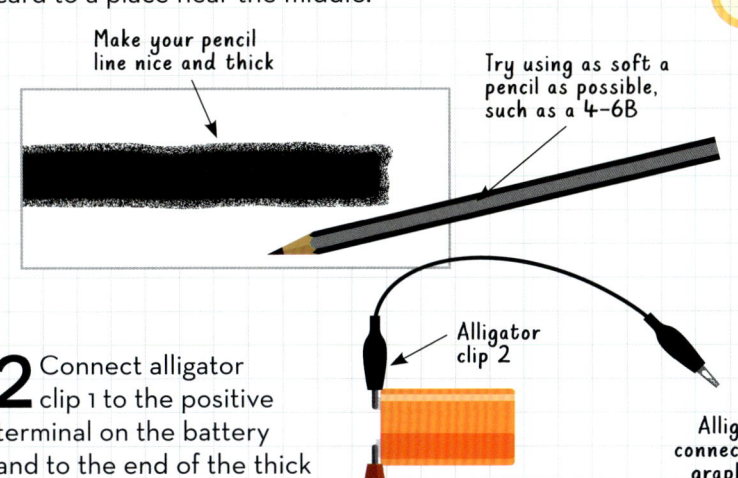

Alligator clip 2

Alligator clip 1

Alligator clip connected to the graphite strip

CURIOUS CURIOSITY

The longest pencil in the world was made by Bic in France and measured a whopping 1,091.99 metres (3,582 ft 7.73 inches) long!

3 Attach the free end of alligator clip 2 to the shorter wire from the LED. Hold the other wire of the LED against the other end of the thick pencil line and see if your LED lights up.

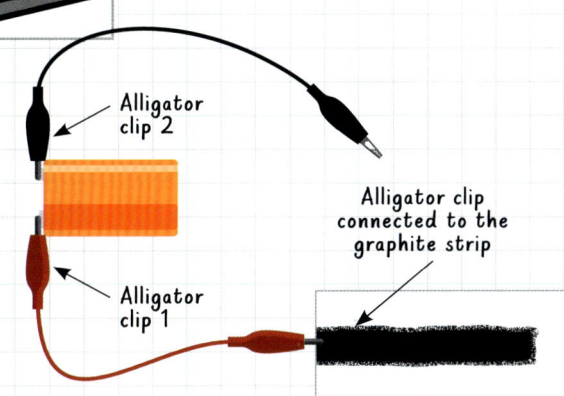

Alligator clip 2

Alligator clip 1

Press the free end of the LED light against the thick pencil line

LED light

What's the SCIENCE?

Grey pencil core is made from graphite, which conducts electricity. It rubs off when you draw a line. The electricity flows along the line you have drawn to complete the circuit.

... TAKE IT FURTHER!

Try making the line longer or thicker. What difference does this make to the brightness of the LED?

25

CONDUCTORS AND INSULATORS

16 SALTY WATER

See how adding salt to water can improve its ability to carry electricity.

WHAT YOU NEED

From the kit:
- Battery holder
- Light globe
- Light-globe holder
- 2 alligator clips

From your home:
- 2 AA batteries
- Plastic bowl
- Salt
- Tape
- Water

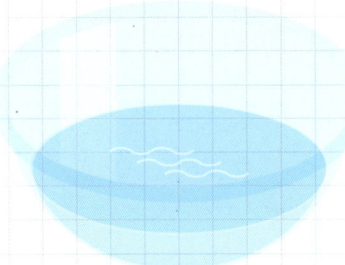

1. Half-fill the bowl with warm water from the tap.

2. Tie one of the wires from the battery holder to one of the connections on the globe holder. Connect alligator clip 1 to the globe holder and put the other end into the water. Connect alligator clip 2 to the other battery holder wire and put the other end into the water.

3. Start adding salt to the bowl, one spoonful at a time. Does the globe start to light up? Stir the water gently to help the salt to dissolve. What happens to the globe?

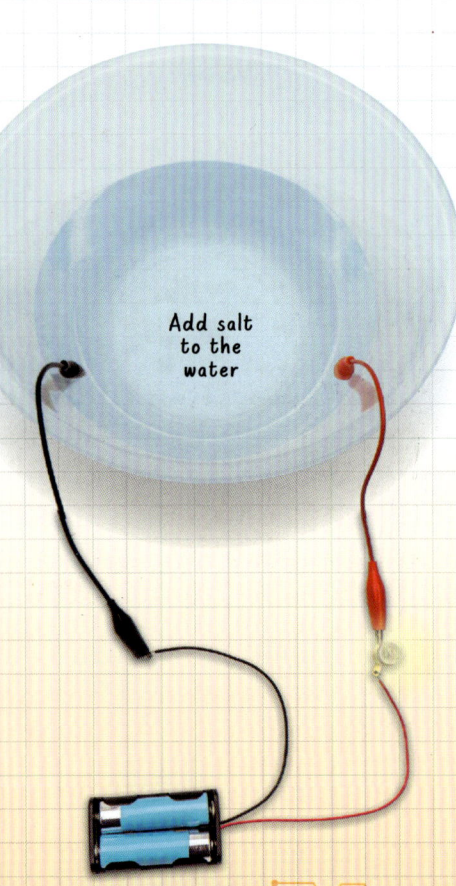

What's the SCIENCE?

Water from the tap does conduct electricity, but adding salt hugely improves its conductivity. The salt molecules split to form sodium ions and chlorine ions, which can move freely with an electric current. The more salt you add, the more current flows and the brighter the bulb will shine. Stirring helps the salt to dissolve – only dissolved salt helps the water to conduct electricity.

CURIOUS CURIOSITY

Seawater contains lots of salt and is a good conductor of electricity. Lightning strikes at sea will electrocute any unfortunate fish that happen to be near the surface, but the water conducts the strike horizontally, so fish that are deeper down stay safe.

CONDUCTORS AND INSULATORS

BUBBLING UP 17

Create tiny bubbles of gas on the tips of pencils using the power of electricity.

WHAT YOU NEED
From the kit:
- Battery holder
- 2 alligator clips

From your home:
- 2 pencils
- Pencil sharpener
- Clear plastic cup or glass beaker
- Tablespoon of salt
- Cardboard

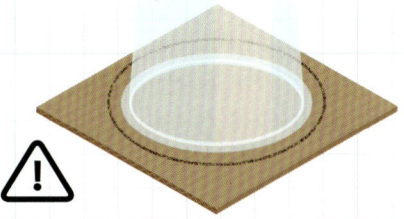

1 Place the cup or glass upside-down on the cardboard and mark a circle roughly 1 cm (0.4 in) outside its edge. Ask an adult to cut out the circle.

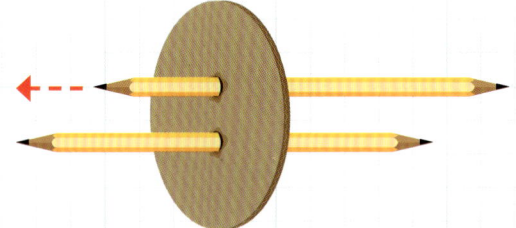

2 Sharpen both ends of the pencils and push them through the card about 1 cm (0.4 in) apart, with half of the length sticking out either side.

3 Fill the glass three-quarters full with warm water and pour a tablespoon of salt into the water. Stir gently until the water becomes clear. Place the card circle over the top of the cup, with the pencil tips in the water.

CURIOUS CURIOSITY
Objects are coated in silver using electrolysis. The object to be coated, such as a metal spoon, is attached to the negative terminal and placed in a solution of silver nitrate. The positive terminal is attached to a piece of silver in the solution.

4 Clip one end of each alligator clip to each pencil core above the card and the other ends to the leads of the battery holder.

5 Watch the pencil cores in the water carefully. After a few seconds, tiny bubbles will appear around each one!

What's the SCIENCE?

You have completed a circuit with the pencils and the salt water. The circuit starts a chemical reaction in the salty water, known as electrolysis. Around the pencil that is attached to the positive terminal on the battery holder, bubbles of chlorine gas appear. Around the pencil that is attached to the negative terminal, bubbles of hydrogen gas appear. The salt in the water, which is a chemical called sodium chloride, turns into the chemical sodium hydroxide.

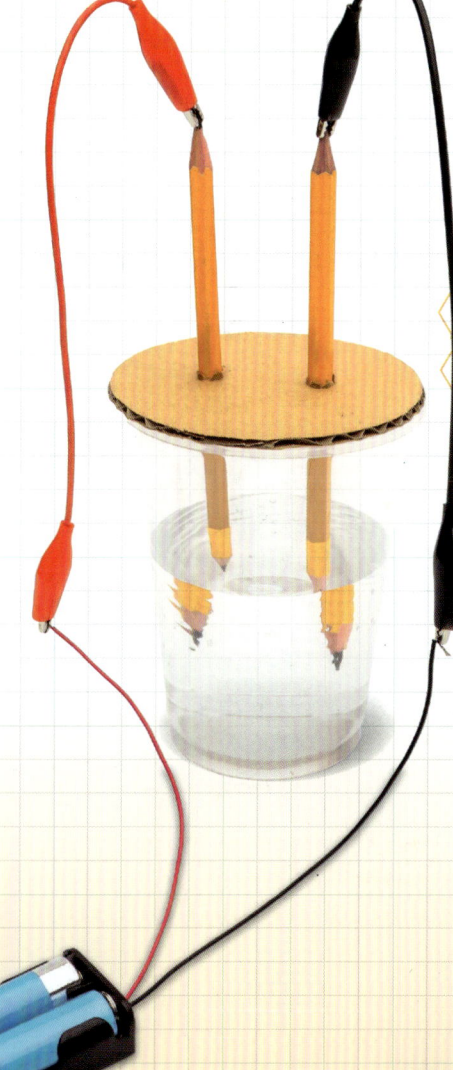

CONDUCTORS AND INSULATORS

18 CONDUCTOR OR INSULATOR?

Test objects around the home to see if they conduct electricity or if they are insulators.

WHAT YOU NEED

From the kit:
- Battery holder
- 3 alligator clips
- Light globe
- Light-globe holder

From your home:
- 2 AA batteries
- A variety of objects

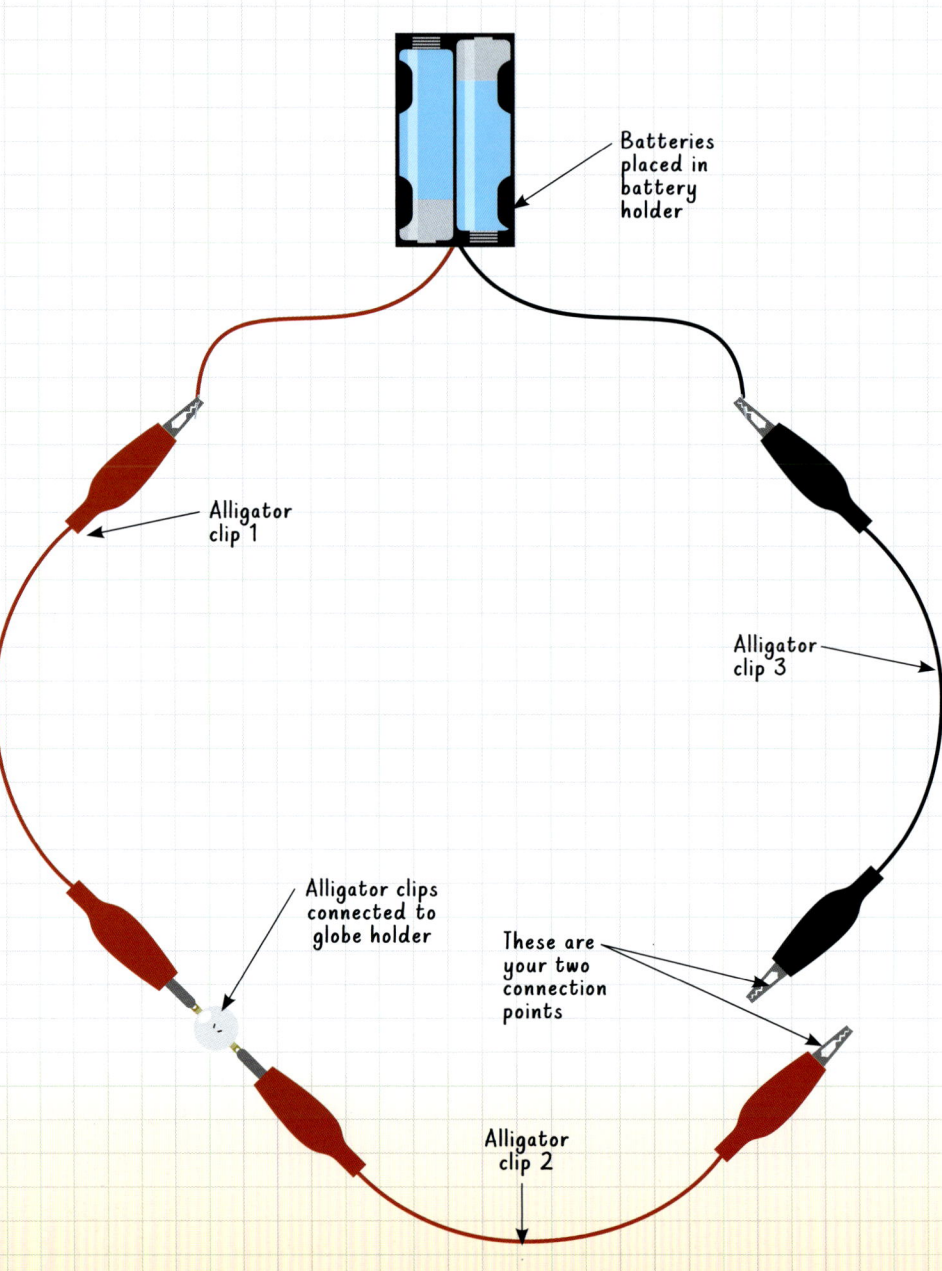

1 Use alligator clip 1 to connect the light globe to the battery holder.

2 Connect alligator clip 2 to the other side of the light-globe holder and connect alligator clip 3 to the other wire of the battery holder.

3 Clip the two free ends of alligator clips 2 and 3 to a variety of household objects. (Don't test electric goods like mobile phones – they may be damaged.) Which ones cause the globe to light up?

CONDUCTORS AND INSULATORS

CURIOUS CURIOSITY

Overhead electricity lines carry powerful electric currents. They are suspended from pylons made of metal – a conductor. The pylons are protected from the power lines by rings made of ceramic, which is a very good insulator. Luckily, the air is also an excellent insulator, so we are perfectly safe down on the ground!

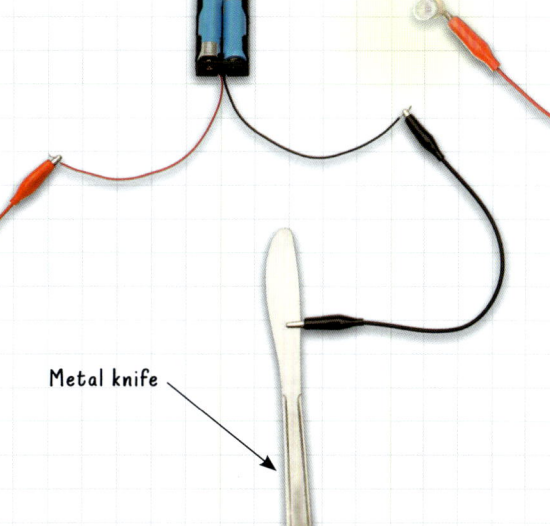

Metal scissors

Metal knife

Scouring pad

What's the SCIENCE?

Any object you connect up that is made of metal, such as a metal knife, will complete the circuit and make the bulb shine. Objects made of insulators, such as plastic, wood or glass, will not complete the circuit. If an object is part-insulator and part-conductor, you will need to connect both alligator clips to the conductor part to complete the circuit.

ELECTROMAGNETS

We use magnets in lots of everyday devices and some of them may surprise you! They help to power speakers on our televisions, store data on our computers and they are even used to look inside our bodies. Magnetism is closely related to electricity. Magnets produce an invisible force that attracts certain materials. When an electric current flows along a wire, it creates a magnetic field around it. An electromagnet is a coiled wire that is magnetised only when an electric current is passed through it.

INDUSTRIAL MAGNETS

Magnets only attract materials known as magnetic materials. These include iron and steel. Powerful electromagnets are used in scrap yards to pick up and drop steel objects such as old cars.

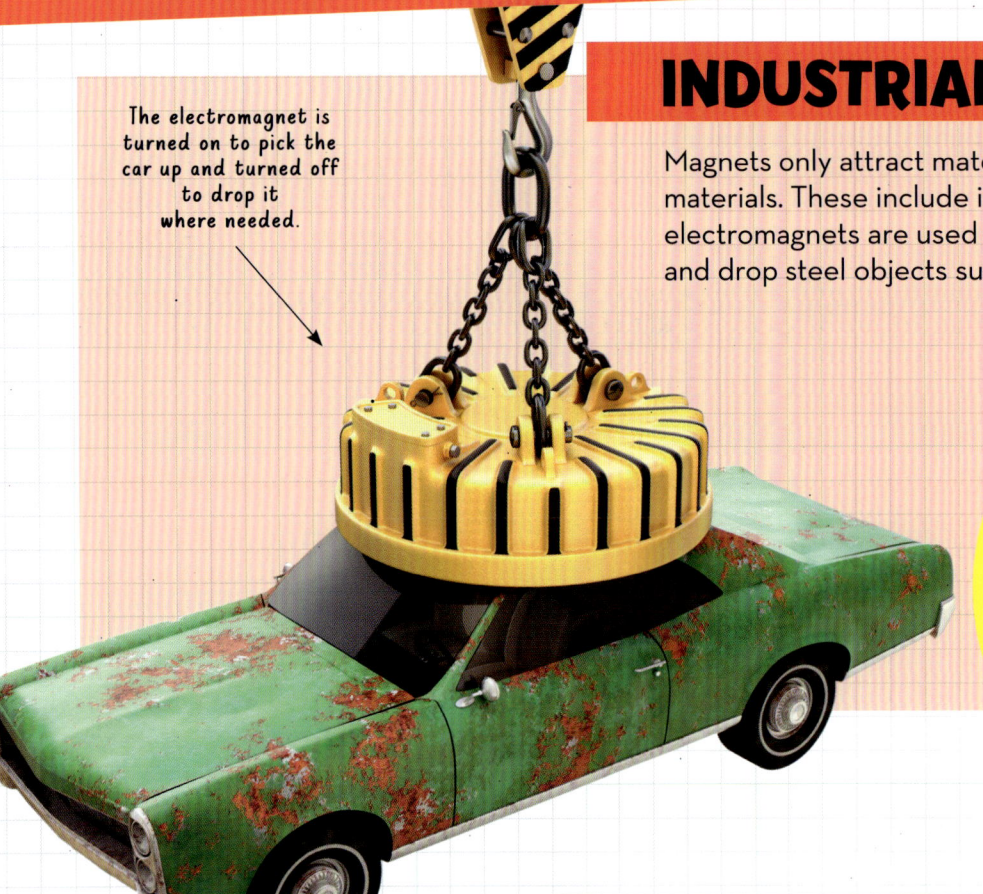

The electromagnet is turned on to pick the car up and turned off to drop it where needed.

PRO-TIP
The strength of an electromagnet increases if there are more coils in the wire. To make your electromagnet stronger, try winding more coils.

MAGNETIC TRAINS

The fastest trains in the world are powered by electromagnets. Maglev trains hover a few inches above a magnetised guideway, where electromagnets pull the train from the front and push it from behind. The fastest maglev train in Japan can zoom along at more than 600 kph (375 mph).

ELECTROMAGNETS

Words you need to know

MAGNETISM
A force that attracts or repels. Magnetism is produced by an electric current.

MAGNETIC FIELD
The area around a magnet in which the force of its magnetism can be detected.

The electric motor in your kit contains a coil of wire which spins in a magnetic field when an electric current runs through it.

MOTORS
Even motors use the power of electromagnetism. A motor produces a spinning motion by passing an electric current through a coil of wire that is free to rotate between permanent magnets. The current produces a magnetic field around the coil, which interacts with the permanent magnets to keep the coil spinning.

MAGNETAR
You must be careful never to hold a debit card (or any other card that stores information) near a magnet as it will erase the information on the card's magnetic strip. The most powerful magnet in the Universe is a kind of star called a magnetar. It could erase the information on a debit card from a distance halfway to the Moon!

Halfway to the Moon equals
192,195 km
(119,425 miles)

GENERATORS
Generators work a little like motors, but in reverse. When a wire moves inside a magnetic field, an electric current starts to flow in the wire. Generators turn a wire coil in a magnetic field. This turns the energy made by the spinning of the coil into electrical energy.

ELECTROMAGNETS

19 COOL COMPASS

Take one cork and one magnet and use the magic magnetic force to make your own homemade compass to find out which way is north.

WHAT YOU NEED

From your home:
- Magnet
- Small bowl
- Cork
- Metal sewing needle
- Pliers
- Knife/hacksaw

WARNING!
You need to be very careful when using magnets. Always use with adult supervision and never swallow them. Magnets can cause serious injury.

⚠ **1** Stroke the magnet along the full length of the sewing needle about a dozen times in the same direction.

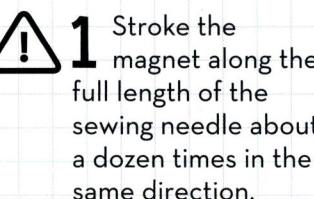
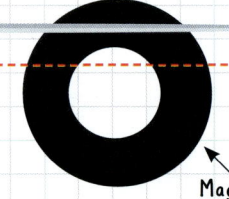

Magnet

⚠ **2** Ask an adult to cut the cork down to make a disc about 1 cm (½ in) thick.

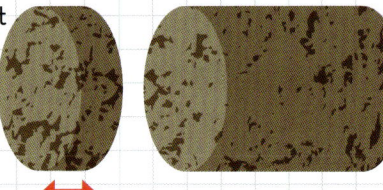

About 1 cm (½ in)

⚠ **3** Ask an adult to push the needle through the cork, holding the needle with the pliers. About the same length of needle should stick out of either side.

Needle

CURIOUS CURIOSITY
Our planet Earth has a magnetic field, which compasses use to show us which direction is north. Many birds use Earth's magnetic field to help them to navigate on long-distance journeys. They sense Earth's magnetism with special substances in their eyes called cryptochromes.

What's the SCIENCE?

Rubbing the needle with the magnet causes the needle to become magnetised. When it spins freely in the water, the needle aligns itself with Earth's magnetic field and points North–South.

... TAKE IT FURTHER!
Hold the magnet close to the pin. Does it turn toward the magnet? You can also hold other metal objects close to it to make it turn.

4 Fill the bowl with a few inches of water and carefully place the cork in the centre of the bowl. Allow it to settle. Check the needle against a compass. What direction does it point in?

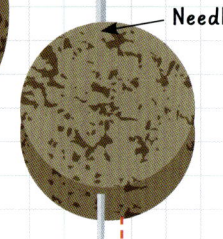

ELECTROMAGNETS

RING IN A SPIN 20

See how magnetism and electricity combine to put a wire into a spin with this simple motor.

WARNING!
You need to be very careful when using magnets. Always use with adult supervision and never swallow them. Magnets can cause serious injury.

WHAT YOU NEED

From the kit:
- 2 alligator clips

From your home:
- Long piece of enamelled copper wire

- Magnet
- 1.5V battery
- 2 large paperclips
- Foam sheet
- Sandpaper

Sandpaper off the enamel on this side

Sandpaper just the top surface on this side

1 Wind the copper wire around to make as many coils as you can. Leave about 5 cm (2 in) of wire on either side. Tightly twist the remaining wire around the coil to hold it together, leaving an inch or so on either side.

2 Using the sandpaper, scrape the enamel off one end of the wire and just the top half of the other end.

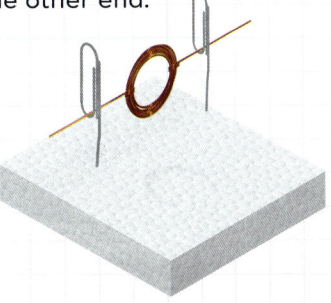

3 Uncoil one side of each paperclip and insert them into the foam sheet so that they are facing one another. They should be close enough that the wire will balance on them.

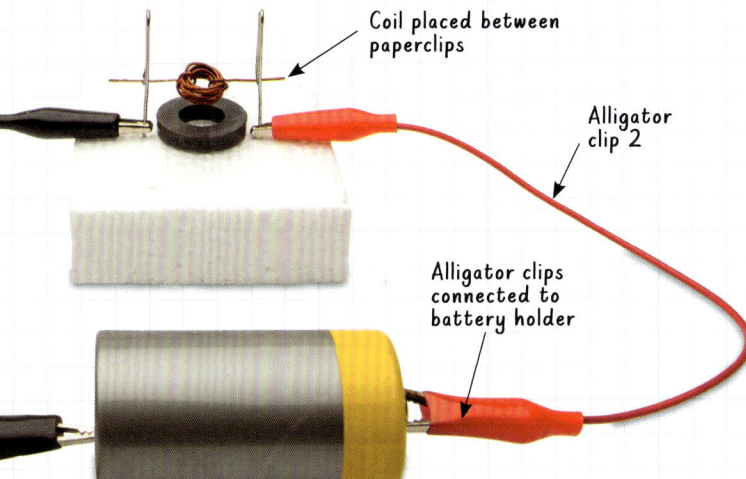
Coil placed between paperclips
Alligator clip 2
Alligator clip 1
Alligator clips connected to battery holder

⚠ 4 Connect the battery to the paperclips with the alligator clips. Place the magnet between the paperclips and insert the coil between the paperclips. Give the coil a nudge to start it turning. It should then spin by itself. If it doesn't start turning, shorten the height of the paperclips a little.

CURIOUS CURIOSITY
The world's smallest electric motor is just one nanometre across – 60,000 of them could fit within the width of a single human hair! The motor is made of just one molecule.

What's the SCIENCE?

Electricity running through the coil creates a magnetic field. This is repelled by the magnet underneath, pushing the coil around. Every half-turn, electricity stops flowing, removing the magnetic field. The coil continues spinning, only to be repelled by the magnet again as the current is switched on one half-turn later.

33

ELECTROMAGNETS

21 ELECTRO-POWER!

Turn an iron nail into a magnet and see what you can pick up with it.

1 Wind the copper wire around the nail about 20 times to form a coil, leaving about 2.5 cm (1 in) free at either end. Use the sandpaper to scrape the enamel from the final 1.5 cm of each end of the wire.

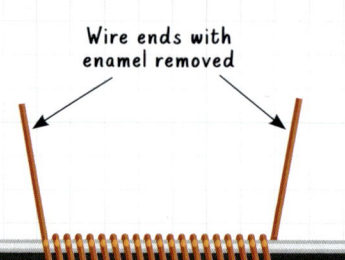
Wire ends with enamel removed

WHAT YOU NEED

From the kit:
- Battery holder
- 2 alligator clips

From your home:
- 1 nail
- Long enamelled copper wire
- 2 AA batteries
- 3 or 4 paperclips
- Sandpaper

The completed circuit makes an electromagnet

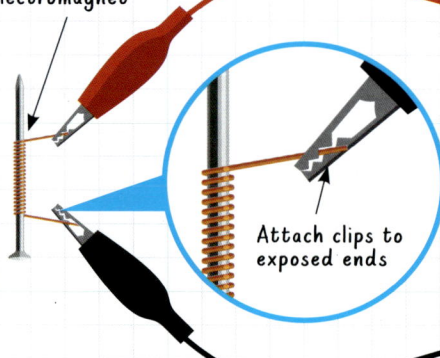
Attach clips to exposed ends

2 Connect alligator clips to the battery holder and the wire ends of your copper wire. This is your electromagnet!

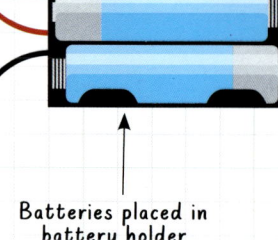
Batteries placed in battery holder

See what other metal items you can pick up

3 Use your electromagnet to pick up the paperclips. How many can you pick up? As soon as you disconnect one of the alligator clips, it will drop the paperclips. Disconnect the electromagnet when you are not using it as it will heat up.

What's the SCIENCE?

The current running through the copper wire creates a magnetic field. This magnetic field magnetises the iron inside it, turning the nail into an electromagnet.

... TAKE IT FURTHER!

The more coils of wire you wind around the nail, the stronger the electromagnet becomes and the heavier the items it can pick up! Try a larger nail and longer wire to make a stronger magnet.

CURIOUS CURIOSITY

In 2008, scientists in Florida built the strongest electromagnet ever. Copper coils were placed inside a cylinder 1.5 m (5 ft) wide and 1.5 m (5 ft) tall to create a magnet two million times more powerful than a fridge magnet.

ELECTROMAGNETS

MORSE CODE MAKER 22

Send secret messages to your friends and communicate in Morse code using this telegraph machine.

1 Wind the copper wire around the nail about 20 times to form a coil, leaving about 2.5 cm (1 in) free at either end. Use the sandpaper to scrape the enamel from the final 1.3 cm (0.5 in) of each end of the wire.

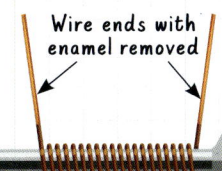
Wire ends with enamel removed

2 Ask an adult to nail the wooden block to one end of the board and hammer the sharp end of the electromagnet into the board in front of the block so that the top of the nail is slightly lower than the top of the block. Then ask an adult to nail the metal strip on top of the block so that it hangs just above the electromagnet.

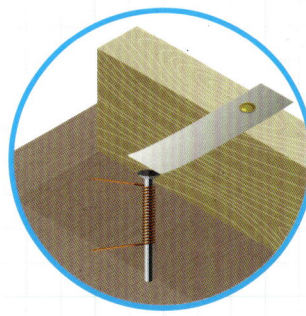

3 Make a switch as you did on page 18. Use the alligator clips to connect the electromagnet to a circuit with the switch and battery.

4 Turn the switch to 'on' and the metal strip will hit the head of the nail and make a clicking sound. Turn it 'off' and then on again to make another click. You've made a Morse code machine! Send messages by varying the time between clicks: short for dot and long for dash. Can you make an SOS signal (... --- ...)?

WHAT YOU NEED

From the kit:
- Battery holder
- 3 alligator clips

From your home:
- Nail
- Long enamelled copper wire
- 2 AA batteries
- A 10-cm (4-in) strip of metal from a steel drinks can
- A block of wood about 10 x 2.5 x 2.5 cm (4 x 1 x 1 in)
- Wooden board • 2 small nails
- Cardboard • Paperclip
- Sandpaper • 2 split pins

CURIOUS CURIOSITY

In 1858, telegraph wires were laid under the Atlantic Ocean to connect North America with Europe. Messages could now be sent in just a few minutes, when before that it took ten days by ship.

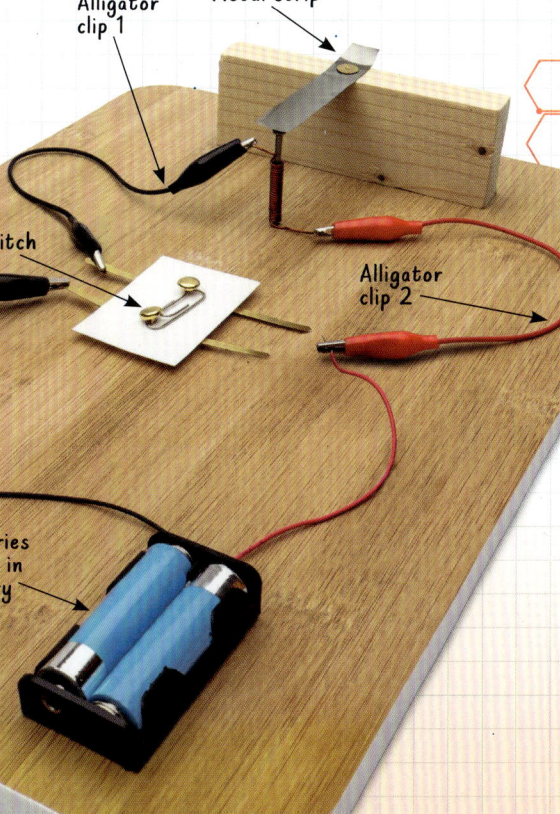

What's the SCIENCE?

When you complete the circuit, the electromagnet pulls the metal strip down to make a click. Disconnect the electromagnet and the strip goes back up again ready for the next click.

ELECTROMAGNETS

23 BUMBLING BRISTLE BOT

Use your electric motor to make a robot with a mind of its own.

WHAT YOU NEED

From the kit:
- Battery holder
- Motor
- 2 alligator clips

From your home:
- 2 AA batteries
- Small brush with no handle
- Modelling clay
- Small bolt or weight

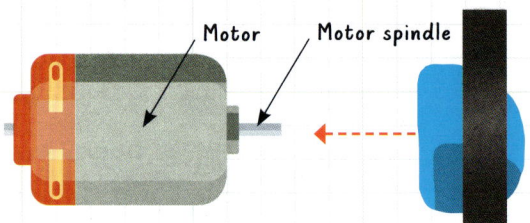

Motor — Motor spindle — Weight fixed to motor spindle with modelling clay then connected to motor spindle

1 Use the modelling clay to attach the bolt or weight to the spindle at one end of your motor.

2 Use some modelling clay to fix the battery holder to one end of the brush. At the other end, secure the motor as shown with another piece of modelling clay.

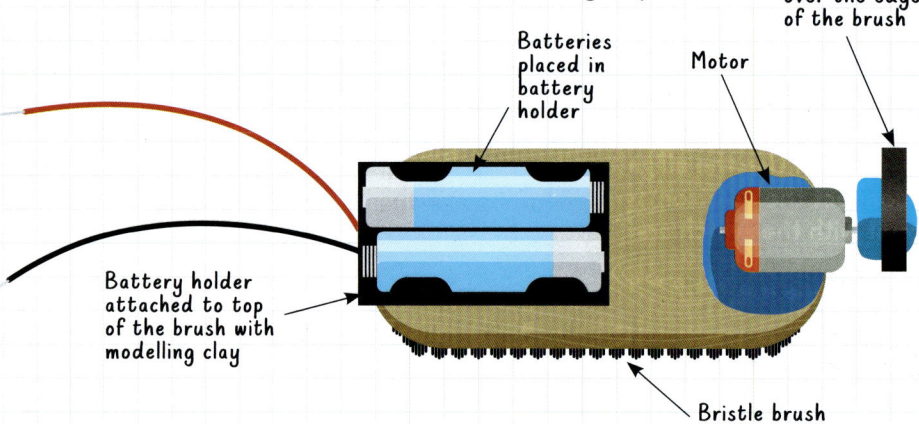

Batteries placed in battery holder
Motor
Make sure the weight hangs over the edge of the brush
Battery holder attached to top of the brush with modelling clay
Bristle brush

CURIOUS CURIOSITY

Robots are often designed to mimic the movements of animals. The US Navy has developed a robot shaped like a tuna, which swims like a fish. Nicknamed 'Ghost Swimmer', it moves in almost complete silence to sneak up on enemy ships.

3 Connect one of the alligator clips to each battery holder lead and the other ends to the terminals on the motor. With the circuit complete, your bristle bot should start moving.

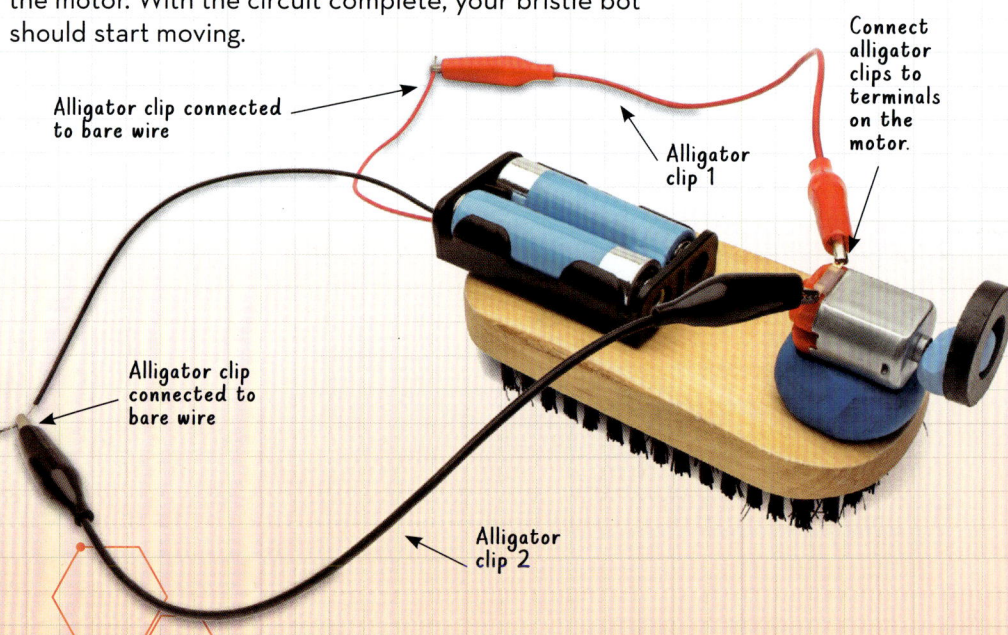

Alligator clip connected to bare wire
Alligator clip 1
Connect alligator clips to terminals on the motor.
Alligator clip connected to bare wire
Alligator clip 2

What's the SCIENCE?

Your bristle bot is moved by the vibrations caused by the motor. The vibrations transfer to the bristles, which push it around. Try angling the motor in different directions to see how this changes the bot's movement.

ELECTROMAGNETS

SEEING THE INVISIBLE 24

WHAT YOU NEED
From your home:
- Bar magnet
- Tube of iron filings
- A4 sheet of white paper
- 2 thin books

WARNING!
You need to be very careful when using magnets and iron filings. Always use with adult supervision and never swallow them. Magnets and iron filings can cause serious injury.

Sprinkle iron filings around a magnet to reveal the shape and size of its invisible magnetic force.

 **1** Place the magnet between the books and place the paper over it with the magnet in the centre.

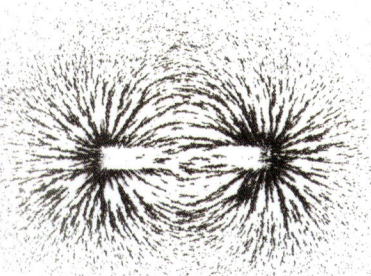

2 Carefully shake the iron filings around the centre of the paper and watch the pattern they arrange themselves into.

The iron filings will follow the shape of the magnetic field

What's the SCIENCE?

The filings are made from iron, which is a magnetic material. They are attracted to the magnetic field around the magnet, arranging themselves along the lines of magnetic force. The magnetic field extends around the magnet from the north to the south poles in three dimensions.

25 WHICH WAY?

Use magnets to make your own simple compass and find out which way is north.

WHAT YOU NEED
From your home:
- 2 small bar magnets
- Pencil • Tape
- Modelling clay
- Craft stick

 1 Tape the magnets to either end of the popsicle stick with the opposite poles facing one another (such as north and south).

Popsicle stick balanced on pencil end so magnets can rotate

2 Push the blunt end of the pencil into a ball of modelling clay so that it stands upright. Place the centre of the popsicle stick on the pointed end of the pencil. Carefully move it around until it is balanced. Give the compass stick some time and it will turn to align itself to north and south.

Pencil pushed into modelling clay which is stuck to table top surface

What's the SCIENCE?

The magnets are lined up so that both of their north poles point in the same direction. They align themselves so that their north poles point toward Earth's south and their south poles point to Earth's north.

37

STATIC ELECTRICITY

STATIC ELECTRICITY

Youch! Have you ever walked across a rug then touched a metal door handle and received an electric shock? This shock is caused by the build-up of a form of electricity known as static electricity.

OPPOSITES ATTRACT

Surfaces with extra electrons have a negative electrical charge, while surfaces with fewer electrons have a positive charge. Like charges repel one another, while opposite charges attract. When you rub a balloon on your sweater, the balloon's surface picks up extra electrons. It will be attracted to an object with positive charge and also to an object with no charge, such as a wall.

SPARKING OFF

Electrical charge can build up on the surface of an object that is a good insulator. It is called 'static' electricity because the charge remains in one place. A build-up of static can lead to a short, sharp flow of electricity in the form of a spark if the electrons have a place to flow to, such as a metal handle.

The balloon will stick to the wall until the electrons have had time to leak away. It won't stick to a conductor such as a metal as the extra electrons will immediately flow away from the surface.

✓ PRO-TIP

The weather can affect your experiments! If it's damp outside, then you might find that some of your static experiments don't work so well, as objects won't hold their charge when things are humid.

STATIC ELECTRICITY

Words you need to know

DISCHARGE
The release of an electrical charge that has built up in one place.

LIGHTNING STRIKE

A bolt of lightning is a spectacular display of the power of static electricity. Electrical charges build up in clouds and they are discharged through the air to the ground in a mighty spark of electricity. A bolt of lightning lasts just a fraction of a second, but it contains enough energy to power a household for a month!

THE TEMPERATURE OF LIGHTNING CAN REACH NEARLY **30,000°C** (54,000°F) – THAT'S FIVE TIMES HOTTER THAN THE SURFACE OF THE SUN.

BAD HAIR DAY

Have you ever noticed that when you take off a hat, it often leaves your hairs standing on end? This is due to static electricity. Some of the electrons in your hair are transferred to your hat, leaving the hairs with a positive charge. Like charges repel, so the hairs try to get as far away from one another as possible.

STATIC ELECTRICITY

26 LEVITATING PLATES!

See how the amazing power of static electricity can turn everyday things into highly charged objects that stick together like glue!

WHAT YOU NEED
From your home:
- Styrofoam plate
- Aluminium pie dish
- Drawing pin
- Pencil with an eraser
- Small piece of yarn

1 Push the drawing pin up through the centre of the pie dish and push the eraser end of the pencil down onto the drawing pin.

Push the pencil down onto the pin so it stands upright

2 Place the Styrofoam plate upside down on a table. Rub the plate as hard as you can with the yarn for about a minute.

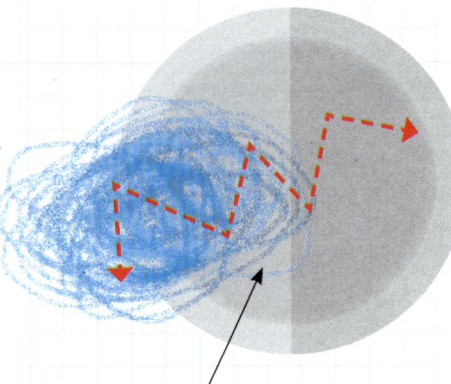

Rub the back of the plate with the yarn

3 Pick up the pie dish using the pencil and place it on top of the plate. **Make sure that you don't touch the dish!** Now lift the pencil and dish, and watch as the plate lifts up with it! Amazing!

CURIOUS CURIOSITY

Lightning is caused by the build-up of static electricity in clouds, with positive charge gathering at the top of the cloud and negative charge at the bottom. The clouds must contain ice for this to happen. Ice particles sink to the bottom of the clouds, gaining a negative charge as they rub against rising water droplets.

What's the SCIENCE?

Rubbing the plate transfers electrons to the surface of the plate, giving it a negative charge. Holding the plate near the dish produces a positive charge in the dish. When you put the dish down onto the plate, they are strongly attracted to one another. When you pull the pencil, this attraction pulls the plate up with the dish.

STATIC ELECTRICITY

STICKY BALLOONS 27

Charge up balloons with static electricity and see where they stick!

WHAT YOU NEED
From your home:
- 2 balloons
- Felt cloth

1 Inflate both balloons and charge just one of them by rubbing it with the felt cloth or on your hair. Now hold the balloons close to one another. Do they stick together?

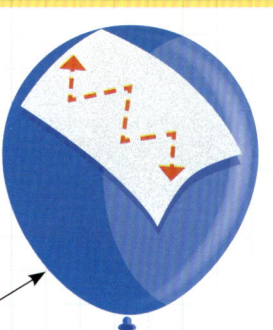
Charged balloon

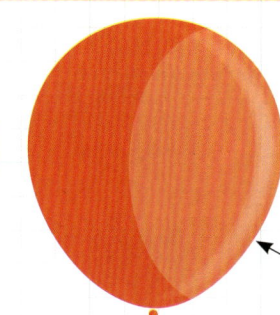
Balloon not charged

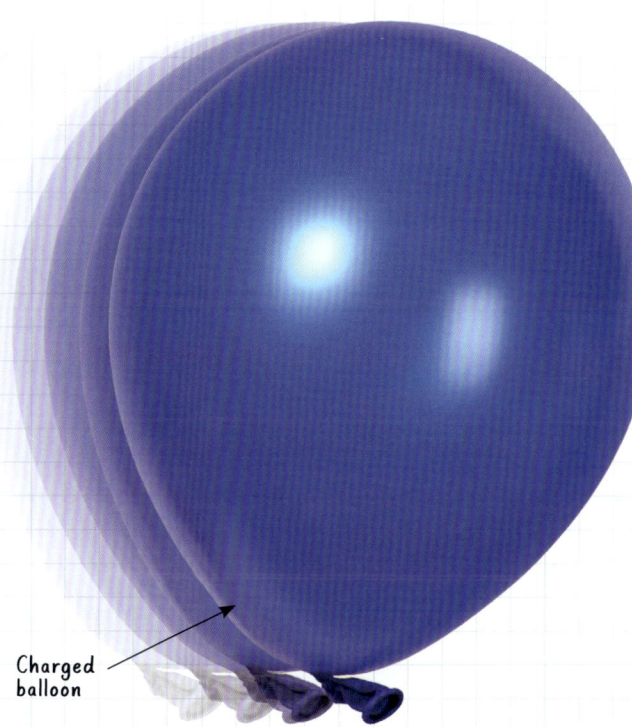
Charged balloon — Charged balloon

2 Charge both balloons and hold them close to one another. Do they attract or repel one another?

CURIOUS CURIOSITY

Did you know that photocopiers and laser printers operate using static electricity? Negatively charged ink is attracted to a positively charged copying plate, which prints the image on a sheet of paper.

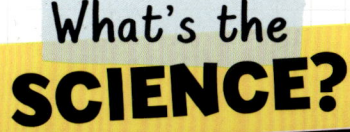

What's the SCIENCE?

Rubbing the balloons creates an excess of electrons on the surface, giving them a negative static electricity charge. A charged balloon will stick to an uncharged balloon, but if you rub both balloons, they will both have negative charge and they will try to push one another away, as like charges repel.

41

STATIC ELECTRICITY

28 PULL THE PEPPER

Use the power of static electricity to sort the salt from the pepper.

WHAT YOU NEED
From your home:
- Salt
- Pepper
- Plastic spoon
- Small tray
- Felt cloth

1. Pour equal amounts of salt and pepper onto the tray and mix them together.

2. Charge the spoon by rubbing it with the felt cloth. *(Rub the felt cloth quickly up and down the spoon)*

3. Hold the spoon above the salt and pepper mixture and slowly lower it down. Watch the pepper jump up onto the spoon.

📌 CURIOUS CURIOSITY
Some factories put a static charge into the smoke coming out of their chimneys, but it's actually for a very smart reason! As the smoke passes electrodes with an opposite charge, the smoke particles are attracted to them before they reach the outside, reducing pollution.

What's the SCIENCE?
The granules of pepper are much lighter than the grains of salt, so they jump up onto the charged spoon, leaving the salt behind. Be careful not to hold the spoon too close to the mixture or the salt will be attracted as well.

STATIC ELECTRICITY

CATCH THE CORN 29

Make your own magical substance that's part liquid, part solid. Then see what static electricity does to it.

WHAT YOU NEED
From your home:
- 50 g (1.78 oz) cornflour
- 50 ml (2 fl oz) vegetable oil
- Small mixing bowl
- Wooden spoon
- Balloon
- Felt cloth

TIP
Before you start, don't forget to cover your work surface. Also, wash your hands before and after the experiment.

Mixed cornflour and oil

1. Pour the cornflour and the vegetable oil into the bowl. Stir the mixture with the spoon until it thickens.

CURIOUS CURIOSITY
Did you know that if you fill a paddling pool with this cornflour mixture, you can run across it without getting your feet wet. The pressure of your footsteps is enough to make it act like a solid for just long enough to take your next step. But keep going! As soon as you stop, you will sink into the goo!

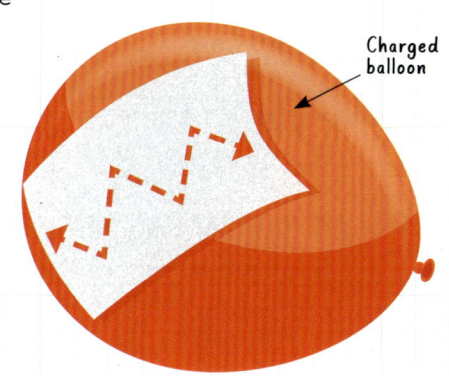
Charged balloon

2. Inflate the balloon and rub it vigorously on the felt cloth or your hair.

3. Take a spoonful of the cornflour mixture and tip it so that it starts to drip off the edge of the spoon. Place the balloon near the spoon. Once you see the cornflour jump toward the balloon, slowly move the balloon away. What happens?

What's the SCIENCE?

This mixture is a substance known as a non-Newtonian fluid or oobleck. It drips like a liquid until it is put under pressure, at which point it starts acting like a solid. The pull from the charged balloon provides enough pressure to turn the cornstarch from a liquid into a solid, making it stop dripping.

STATIC ELECTRICITY

30 JIGGLY JELLAGMITES

WHAT YOU NEED

From your home:
- Balloon
- Gelatin mix
- A3 sheet of paper
- Felt cloth

See how you can use static electricity to craft some crazy stalagmites of gelatin.

1. Spread the dry gelatin mix evenly over the sheet of paper.

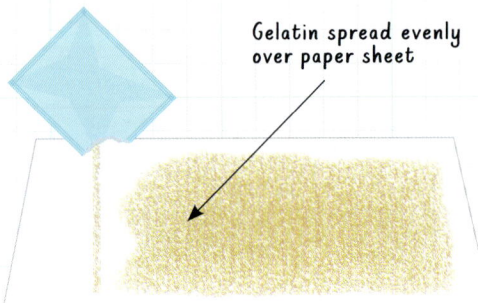

Gelatin spread evenly over paper sheet

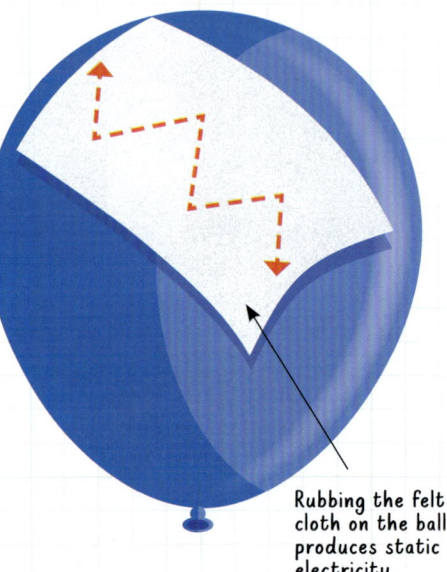

Rubbing the felt cloth on the balloon produces static electricity

2. Charge the balloon by rubbing it with the felt cloth.

3. Hold the balloon over the gelatin. You will need to get very close and perhaps even touch the gelatin. Slowly raise the balloon to create long, thin stalagmites of gelatin rising up and perhaps also some stalactites hanging down from the balloon.

CURIOUS CURIOSITY

In caves, spikes of minerals called stalagmites and stalactites often form in pairs. Stalactites form from the minerals left behind by water dripping from the roof. Stalagmites form on the floor where the drops of water fall. Eventually, they may join in the middle to form columns!

TIP
Before you start, don't forget to cover your work surface. Also, wash your hands before and after the experiment.

What's the SCIENCE?

The negatively charged balloon attracts the particles of gelatin powder, lifting them up. This experiment also works with sugar, but the particles of sugar are heavier so the stalagmites do not last as long.

Gelatin stalactites on the balloon surface

Gelatin stalagmites on the paper surface

STATIC ELECTRICITY

BEND THE FLOW 31

WHAT YOU NEED
From your home:
- Comb
- Tap

Bend a stream of water with a static-charged comb.

1 Charge the comb by running it through your hair several times. The more times you comb, the more bending strength it will have.

2 Hold the comb near a thin stream of water flowing from the tap and watch the stream bend towards it.

Slowly turn the tap on so you have a thin flow of running water

Move the comb back slowly

What's the SCIENCE?
The stream of water is attracted to the charged comb.

32 LOOK, NO HANDS!

Static electricity can move objects without touching them – see this in action!

WHAT YOU NEED
From your home:
- Balloon
- Empty metal drink can
- Felt cloth

1 Inflate and charge the balloon by rubbing it with your felt cloth.

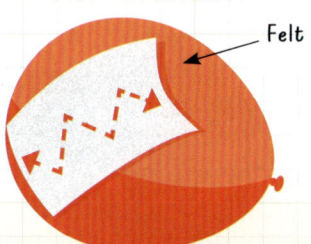

Felt cloth

Charged balloon

2 Place the can on its side on a tabletop or the ground and hold the balloon close to it. Now move the balloon to start the can rolling!

What's the SCIENCE?
The can is attracted to the negatively charged balloon. The can will roll when it is empty because it is very light. The static charge will not be strong enough to move it if it is full.

45

BATTERIES

How would you like to carry around the power of electricity in your pocket? Well guess what? You probably already do! Batteries produce electricity by converting chemical energy into electrical charges that flow when they are connected to a circuit.

CONTENTS OF A BATTERY

A battery contains three parts:

1. the negative electrode (anode) is the end of the battery from which electrons flow
2. the positive electrode (cathode) is the end of the battery toward which electrons flow
3. the electrolyte is a chemical that separates the positive and negative electrodes.

When the battery is connected to a circuit, chemical reactions occur between the electrolyte and the electrodes. Electrons are removed from atoms to leave positive ions. The ions move toward the cathode. The electrons move toward the anode. The electrons flow around the circuit and recombine with the ions at the cathode. In science, a single unit is technically called a cell, while a battery is a group of cells, but we commonly refer to a cell as a battery.

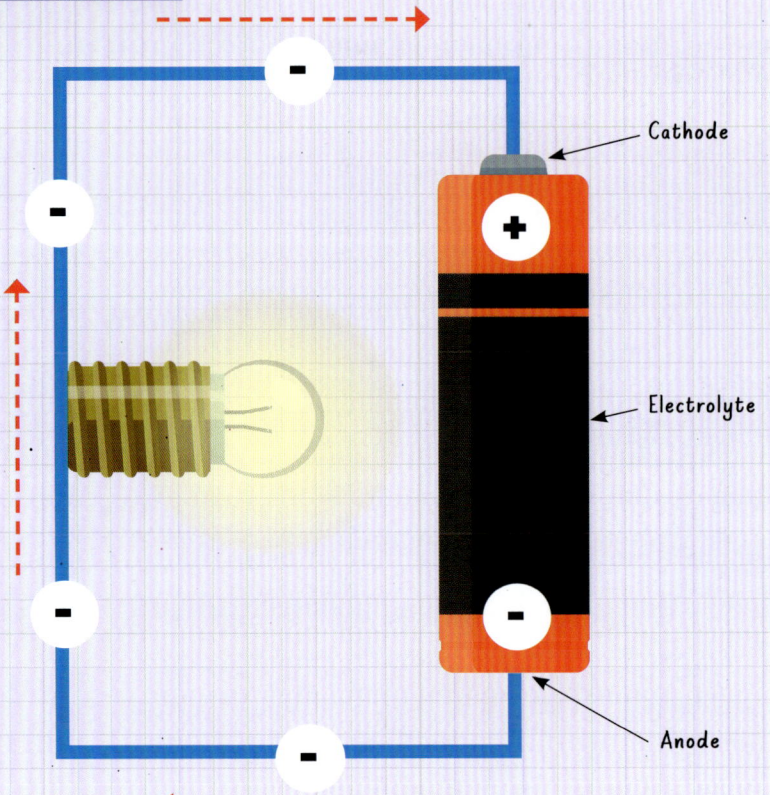

PRO-TIP
For the projects with copper coins, you can use silver coins instead if you do not have copper coins in your country. 'Silver' coins are made from a mix of copper and nickel and they work almost as well.

REVERSING THE PROCESS
In time, the chemical reaction in the electrolyte stops and the battery dies. In rechargeable batteries, the chemical reaction can be reversed by running electricity back through the battery.

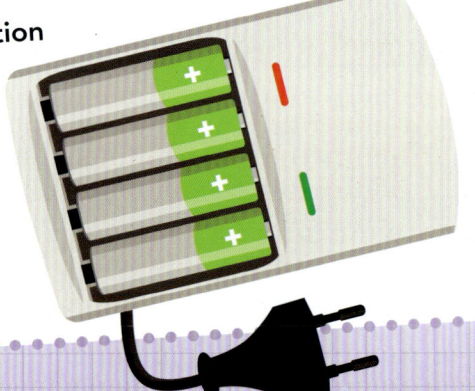

BATTERIES

Words you need to know

ELECTROLYTE
A substance in which current is carried by the movement of ions.

NEGATIVE ELECTRODE
The end of a battery from which electrons flow. It is also called the anode.

POSITIVE ELECTRODE
The end of a battery toward which electrons flow. It is also called the cathode.

GIANT BATTERY

The world's biggest battery was built in 2017 in Jamestown, South Australia. The size of a soccer field, it produces enough electricity to power 30,000 homes. The battery is recharged using energy from a wind farm.

THE FIRST BATTERY

Italian scientist Alessandro Volta invented the battery in 1799. Called a voltaic pile, the first battery was made of a series of alternating copper and zinc plates separated by cloth soaked in salty water. The salty water was the electrolyte, the copper was the positive electrode and the zinc was the negative electrode. The more plates Volta added to his pile, the stronger the current he produced.

The unit for electric charge, the volt, is named after Alessandro Volta

Copper and zinc plates

Paper or leather cloth soaked in salty water

47

BATTERIES

33 POTATO POWER!

Did you know a potato can produce electricity? This project will show you how you can use the humble potato to power electrical gadgets like an LCD clock.

WHAT YOU NEED

From the kit:
- LCD clock
- 4 alligator clips

From your home:
- 3 galvanised nails
- 3 potatoes
- 3 clean copper coins

1 Carefully push a nail and copper coin into each of the potatoes, making sure that you keep the nails and coins in the correct orientation, as shown.

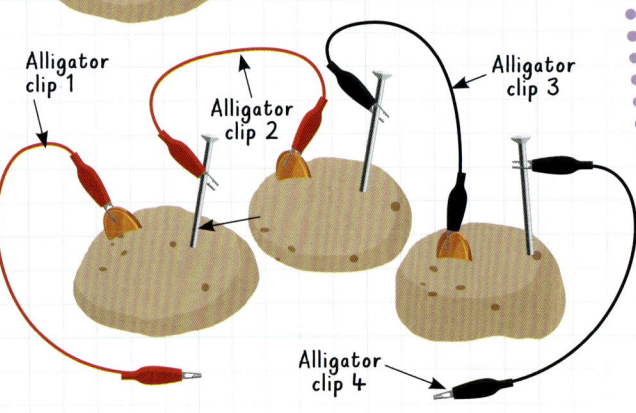

2 Attach alligator clip 1 to the copper coin on the first potato. Attach alligator clip 2 to the nail on the first potato and the coin on the second potato. Attach alligator clip 3 to the nail on the second potato and the coin on the third potato. Attach alligator clip 4 to the nail on the third potato.

3 Connect the free clips on alligator clips 1 and 4 to the wires on the LCD clock. You're done! You should now have a working clock powered by a potato. If the clock hasn't worked, try swapping the wires and connections over.

CURIOUS CURIOSITY

In September 2010, Peter Glazebrook of Nottinghamshire, UK, planted his name in the Guinness World Record books by growing the world's largest potato, which weighed in at just under 4 kg (8.8 lb)! That would power the clock for a very long time!

What's the SCIENCE?

A battery needs two pieces of metal, the electrodes and a fluid (the electrolyte), so that a chemical reaction takes place to make a current. In our potato experiment, the electrodes are the copper coin and nail, while the liquid in the juicy potato acts as the electrolyte.

BATTERIES

ICE TRAY BATTERY 34

Make a multi-cell battery with vinegar in an ice tray. This battery uses the energy in vinegar to light up an LCD. Create a multi-cell battery to give it the greatest possible power.

WHAT YOU NEED

From the kit:
- LED globe

From your home:
- 6 galvanised nails
- Ice cube tray
- Vinegar
- 6 lengths of copper wire each about 12 cm (5 in) long

1 Wrap a length of copper wire around the top of each nail, leaving a length of wire hanging down from each.

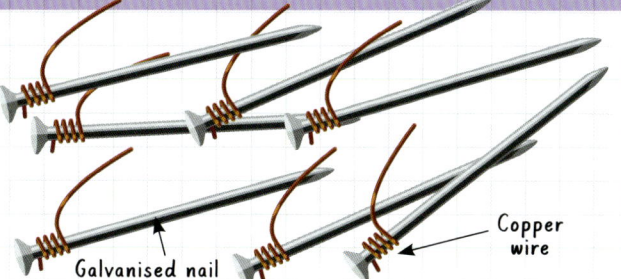

Galvanised nail — Copper wire

2 Fill the first six compartments of the ice tray with vinegar. These will become the cells of your battery.

3 Straddle the wires of the LED globe across the first two cells. Place a nail in one of these cells, with the copper from it dangling into the next cell. Place a nail in this cell and repeat around the cells, as shown, to complete the circuit. Does the LED globe glow?

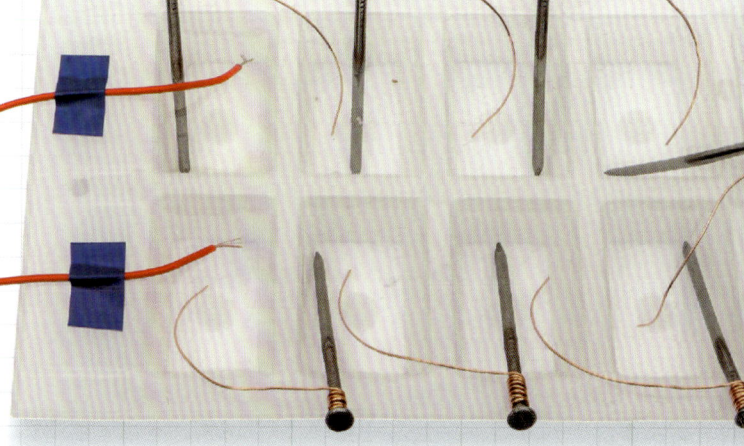

CURIOUS CURIOSITY

A single lithium battery cell can produce voltages of up to 3.7 volts. Machines called Van de Graaff generators can achieve up to 25 million volts. They are used in nuclear physics experiments.

What's the SCIENCE?

A reaction between the acid in the vinegar, the copper in the wires and the zinc that coats the galvanised nails produces an electric current. The cells are connected to one another in series and this produces a larger voltage than one cell on its own. The more cells you connect to your battery, the greater the voltage will be.

BATTERIES

35 MAGNETIC TRAIN

Make an amazing train out of just a battery and some magnets and run it through your copper wire track.

WHAT YOU NEED

From your home:
- AA battery
- 10-m (30-ft) length of thin copper wire
- 4 crafting magnets – the magnets should have a diameter slightly larger than the diameter of the battery

1 Wind the wire into a coil tube to make your track. Make sure that the coils are tightly packed and that the tube is a little wider than the battery – you could wind the wire around a cork to help.

2 Place two magnets on either end of the battery, so that the same poles are facing outward at each end.

The battery and magnets may get hot so be careful when removing

WARNING!
You need to be very careful when using magnets and batteries. Always use with adult supervision and never swallow them. Magnets and batteries can cause serious injury.

CURIOUS CURIOSITY

Crafting magnets are made from a metal called neodymium. Neodymium is excellent for creating very small, very strong permanent magnets. It is used in headphones, microphones and hearing aids – anything that needs light but strong magnets.

3 Insert the battery at one end of the track and watch it zoom to the other end. As the battery train is in the track, join the ends of the track up to one another to form a circle. The battery will continue to zoom around and around.

Adjust the shape of your coil to see what shape works best to propel the battery around the track smoothly

What's the SCIENCE?

An electric current flows from one end of the battery to the other through the magnets and the coil. This turns the coil into an electromagnet just for the length between each end of the train. At one end, the electromagnet and the crafting magnet repel one another, while at the other end, they pull against one another. This pushes the train from the back and pulls it from the front.

BATTERIES

THE POWER OF MONEY 36

Turn the jingling loose change in your pocket into your very own source of electrical power!

WHAT YOU NEED

From the kit:
- LCD clock
- 2 alligator clips

From your home:
- Aluminium foil
- 9 copper coins
- 2 pieces of copper wire
- A4 sheet of card
- Vinegar • Pencil
- Tape • Bowl • Soapy water
- Paper towel • Scissors

1 Clean the coins in a little soapy water and dry them with a paper towel.

3 Draw around one of the coins on the card to make nine coin-shaped circles. Cut the circles out and soak them in a bowl of vinegar.

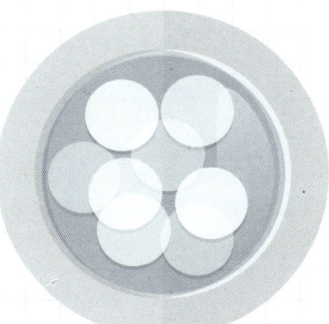

⚠ 2 Cut out nine small discs from the aluminium foil – each disc should be very slightly bigger than one of the coins.

4 Build your battery by first placing down a coin, then carefully placing a piece of card on top and a piece of foil on top of that. Repeat the process, but take care that the foil does not fold down the side to touch other layers. **This is important!**

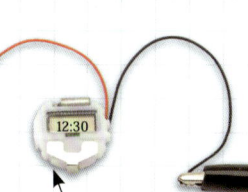

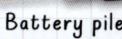

Alligator clip 1 — LCD clock — Alligator clip 2

5 Tape the copper wires to the top and bottom of the battery pile and tape all around your battery pile so that you can pick it up. Use the alligator clips to connect each wire to the LCD clock. Does your clock start working?

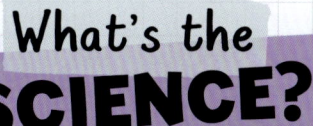
Battery pile

CURIOUS CURIOSITY

Due to the soaring price of copper, mints around the world have changed the composition of coins, coating cheaper metals with a thin layer of copper. In the USA, old pennies contain 95 per cent copper and the metal in them is now worth a lot more than a penny. A law was passed to stop people from melting them down!

What's the SCIENCE?

You have recreated Alessandro Volta's original battery pile! The vinegar acts as the electrolyte, the copper coin is the cathode, while the aluminium foil is the anode. Each set of coin, card and foil is one cell.

BATTERIES

37 LEMON CLOCK

They may taste sour, but lemons can be used to power your clock.

WHAT YOU NEED
From the kit:
- 4 alligator clips
- LCD clock

From your home:
- 3 galvanised nails
- 3 lemons
- 3 clean copper coins

1 Roll the lemons on a hard surface, being careful not to break the skin. This will break up the cells and make them nice and juicy inside.

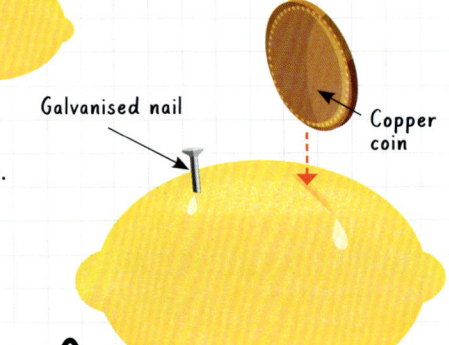

2 Jam one nail and one coin into each lemon. Connect alligator clip 1 to the coin in one lemon and the nail in the next. Connect alligator clip 2 to the coin in the second lemon and the nail in the third.

CURIOUS CURIOSITY

Lemons are very acidic, but they are perfectly safe to eat – the acids in our stomachs are ten times more acidic than lemon juice. However, the liquid inside batteries such as car batteries is ten times more acidic than our stomachs and you should never touch a battery that has been opened up.

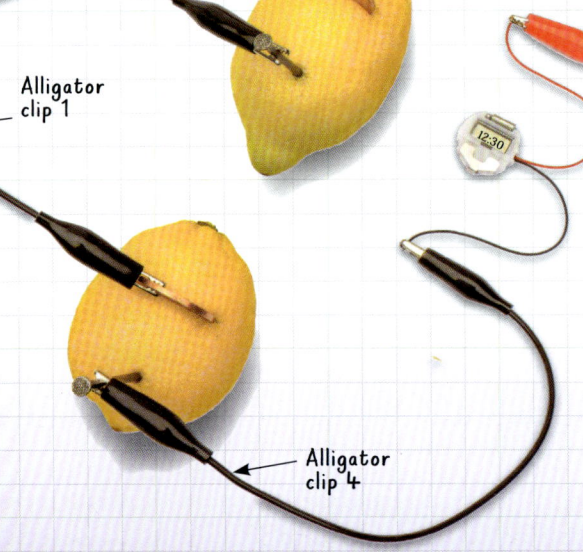

What's the SCIENCE?

You have created a three-cell battery! A chemical reaction between the metals and the citric acid inside the lemon produces the electric current. The nail acts as the negative terminal and the coin as the positive terminal, while the acidic juice of the lemon is the electrolyte. After a few hours, the metals will start to corrode from the chemical reaction and your battery will stop working.

3 Use the other two alligator clips to connect the first and third lemons to the connections on the clock. Give it a few seconds for the chemical reaction to start and the LCD display should light up.

BATTERIES

SALTY BATTERY 38

WHAT YOU NEED

From the kit:
- 3 alligator clips
- LCD clock

From your home:
- 2 galvanised nails
- 2 clean copper coins
- Salt
- 2 plastic cups
- Tape • Tablespoon

Make a battery out of salt water and use it to power your clock.

1 Half-fill the cups with warm water and add a couple of tablespoons of salt to each cup. Stir well so that all the salt dissolves. Tape a nail to one side of each cup and a coin to the other side so that they are part-submerged in the water, as shown.

2 Connect the nail of one cup to the coin of the other with an alligator clip and connect the spare nail and coin to the LCD clock. The clock will come on after a few seconds.

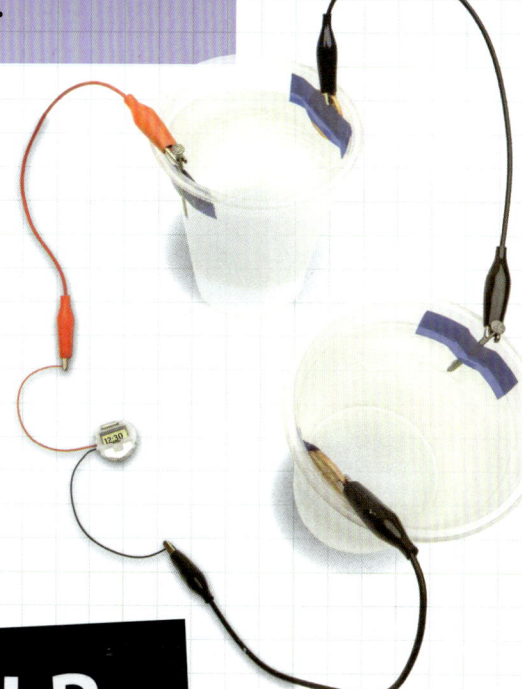

What's the SCIENCE?

You have made a two-cell battery! You can make a stronger one by adding more cups of salty water.

39 BATTERY AND BULB

Light a bulb from a battery using only one wire.

1 Attach one end of the alligator clip to the positive end of the battery and the other end to a connector on the globe holder. Now, holding the alligator clip by the plastic head, touch the bulb to the negative end of the battery. It will light up brightly.

WHAT YOU NEED

From the kit:
- Alligator clip
- Light globe
- Light-globe holder

From your home:
- AA battery

- Alligator clip connected to the positive terminal on the battery
- Alligator clip connected to one side of the globe holder
- Light globe screwed into globe holder

What's the SCIENCE?

You complete the circuit by touching the bulb to the negative terminal and break it when you take it away.

53

SOLAR POWER

SOLAR POWER

Every second of every day, Earth is bombarded by energy from the sun. Solar panels harness this energy to produce electricity. Solar power is an example of a clean, renewable energy source – a source of energy that does not run out and does not produce pollution.

ENERGY CELLS

Solar panels contain parts called photovoltaic cells. These cells use the energy from light to build up an electric charge. The technology behind solar panels is improving quickly. The latest developments include transparent cells that can turn a pane of glass into a solar panel. Buildings of the future may be powered by their windows!

PRO-TIP

The solar panel in this kit works in direct sunlight or when held close to a light bulb. Some energy-saving light bulbs are not bright enough, so you may need to try different ones.

POWER FROM SPACE

Solar panels on Earth can only gather energy during daylight and much of the light is often blocked by clouds. In space, the panels on satellites can face the sun directly nearly 24 hours a day. In 2015, the Japan Aerospace Exploration Agency beamed energy from a solar panel in space down to Earth in the form of microwaves. In the future, solar panels in orbit may provide us with a source of reliable, continuous renewable energy.

SOLAR POWER

RENEWABLES

Solar power is one form of cheap, endless energy that is good for the environment, but there are others too!

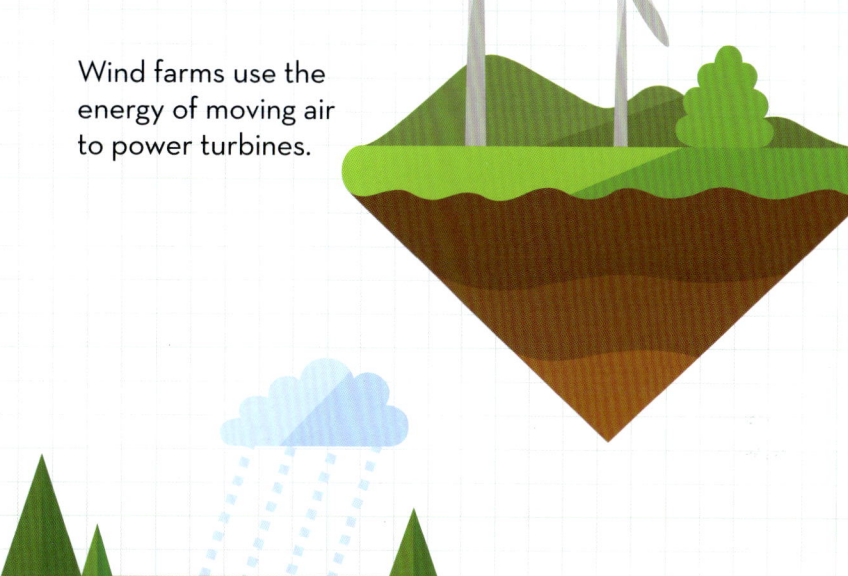

Wind farms use the energy of moving air to power turbines.

Hydroelectricity is generated using moving water.

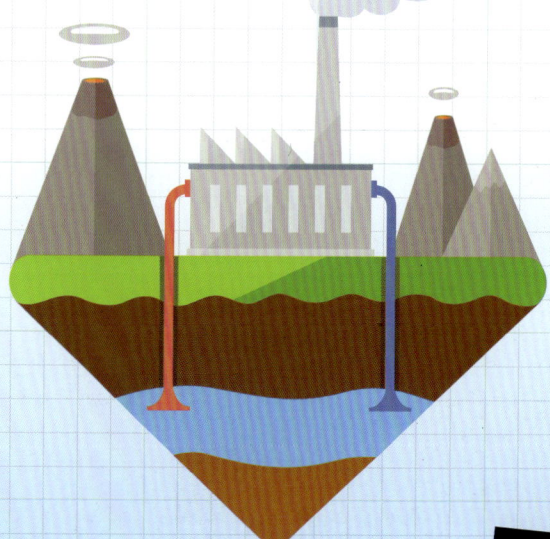

Geothermal power plants send water through pipes to be heated by hot underground rocks. This turns the water into steam, which powers the turbines.

Words you need to know

MICROWAVE
A form of energy that is similar to visible light. Microwaves have longer wavelengths than visible light and are invisible to our eyes.

TURBINE
A bladed wheel that is turned by the power of a moving liquid or gas, such as water or steam.

31 PER CENT OF THE WORLD'S ENERGY COMES FROM RENEWABLE SOURCES.

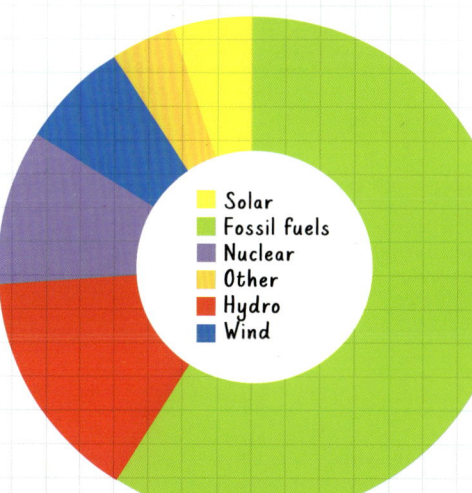

- Solar
- Fossil fuels
- Nuclear
- Other
- Hydro
- Wind

59 PER CENT OF THE WORLD'S ENERGY COMES FROM FOSSIL FUELS, SUCH AS COAL AND OIL.

10 PER CENT COMES FROM NUCLEAR POWER.

SOLAR POWER

40 SOLAR BOAT

WHAT YOU NEED
From the kit:
- Solar panel and motor

From your home:
- A4 piece of foam sheet
- Small piece of card
- Tape

Make this mini solar-powered boat and watch it float along in the sunlight.

⚠ **1** Ask an adult to use a sharp knife to sculpt the hull for your boat from the foam sheet. Make it about 2 cm (1 in) thick, 5 cm (2 in) wide and 8 cm (3 in) long, with a pointed front. Tape a small block of foam about 2 cm (1 in) high to the back of the hull.

CURIOUS CURIOSITY

When it was built in 2006, the container ship *Emma Maersk* was the biggest ship in the world. Its propeller is 9.6 m (31.5 ft) in diameter. Cast from bronze, it weighs 130 tons.

⚠ **2** Trace the shape below onto the card and ask an adult to cut it out. Cut along the solid lines and score and bend along the dashed lines to make your propeller blades.

3 Tape the solar panel to the top of the hull and the motor to the back block, with the spindle pointing backwards.

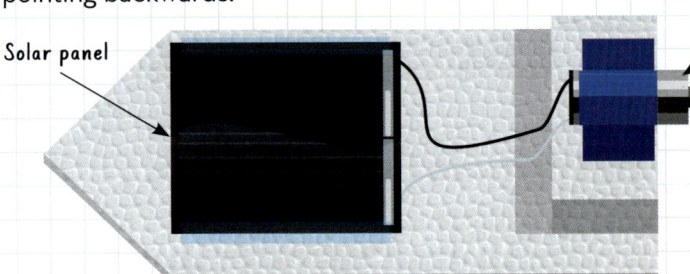

Solar panel

Motor power turns the propeller

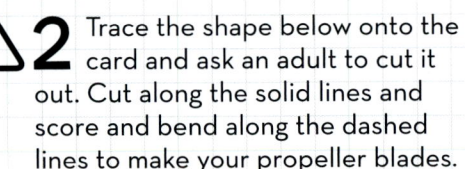

PROPELLER TEMPLATE

Cut here
Score here

4 Stick a small piece of tape across the centre of both sides of the propeller and attach it to the spindle of the motor with the blades angled backwards. Place your solar boat on water in the sun or under a lamp.

Propeller held both sides with tape

Solar panel taped to top of boat

What's the SCIENCE?

The motor spins the propeller. The propeller is shaped like a section of a screw and turns the spinning motion into a force that pushes the air backwards. This in turn pushes the boat forward.

56

SOLAR POWER

UPDRAFT TOWER 41

Make a pinwheel spin with the warming energy of the sun.

⚠ **1** Ask an adult to cut off the bottom of the tube. Wrap aluminium foil around the outside of the tube and tape it in place. The foil will reflect sunlight and stop the tower from heating up.

2 Bend the length of poseable wire into the shape shown. Attach a small blob of modelling clay to the middle at the top.

WHAT YOU NEED

From your home:
- Long cardboard tube, such as a Pringles® container
- 2 books of the same size
- Square sheet of paper
- Drawing pin
- Poseable wire 10 cm (4 in) long
- Tape
- Aluminium foil
- Modelling clay

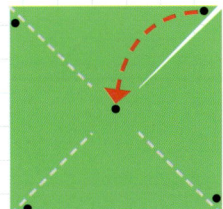 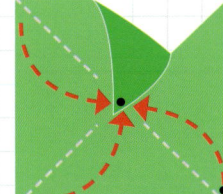 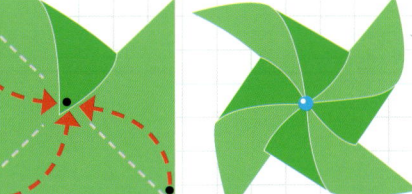

3 Make a pinwheel from the paper. Begin with a square of paper. Fold your square, corner to corner, then unfold. Make a pencil mark about ⅓ of the way from the centre. Cut along the fold lines. Bring each point into the centre and stick the drawing pin through all four points.

4 Attach the pinwheel to the modelling clay at the top of the tower with its cups pointing down and the drawing pin facing up. Place your tower in direct sunlight resting on the two books with a gap between them. Does the wheel start to spin?

Add a blob of modelling clay to the drawing pin point to keep your pinwheel in place

CURIOUS CURIOSITY

There are plans to build a giant updraft tower 1 km (0.6 miles) high in Australia. The rising air will power turbines to generate electricity.

What's the SCIENCE?

The tower works on the simple principle that hot air rises. The heat from the sun warms the air at the bottom of the tower. This warm air rises through the tower to turn the pinwheel.

Make sure the gap between the books at the bottom is as wide as possible to allow air to go up the tube

SOLAR POWER

42 SOLAR RAINBOW WHEEL

Use the power of the sun to produce this magical wheel and watch it change colour in front of your eyes.

WHAT YOU NEED
From the kit:
- Solar panel and motor

From your home:
- A4 sheet of cardboard
- Colour crayons
- Modelling clay

⚠ 1. Ask an adult to cut out a cardboard circle about 5 cm (2 in) in diameter. Divide the circle into quarters and use the crayons to colour in the wheel, with blue opposite yellow and red opposite green.

CURIOUS CURIOSITY

Light comes in a range of wavelengths known as the electromagnetic spectrum. We see different wavelengths as colours, but we can only detect a narrow band of the spectrum. Many birds can see ultraviolet, which has a shorter wavelength than the light we can see. The world is even more colourful to birds than it is to us.

2. Press a small blob of modelling clay on to the centre of the back of the card. Attach the centre of the card to the spindle of the motor, using the modelling clay to hold it in place.

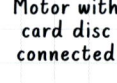
Motor with card disc connected

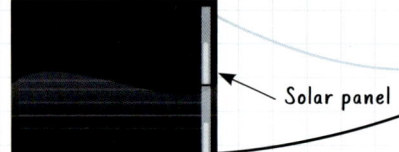
Solar panel

3. Place the solar panel in sunlight or under a desk lamp to start the wheel spinning. Watch as the colours appear to change.

What's the SCIENCE?

Spinning the colour wheel quickly fools our eyes into believing that we are seeing all the colours at the same time across the whole wheel. We see this mix of colours as white light. The more different colours you add to the wheel, the purer the white light will appear.

... TAKE IT FURTHER!
Make a wheel using all the colours of the rainbow: red orange, yellow, green, blue, indigo and violet.

SOLAR POWER

SOLAR SNACKS 43

Heat up a pizza with this solar oven, which concentrates the power of sunlight.

⚠ **1** Ask an adult to cut a flap in the lid of the pizza box with a sharp knife. Cut along three sides, leaving about 3 cm (1 in) around the edge.

2 Open the flap of your box and cover the inner side of the flap with aluminium foil, tightly wrapping the foil around the flap and taping it in place on the outer side.

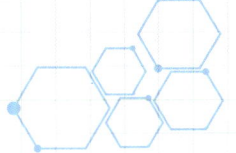

Score along this edge to make your folding flap

WHAT YOU NEED
From your home:
- Empty pizza box
- Aluminium foil
- Clear tape
- Plastic wrap
- Black paper
- Newspaper
- Metal or wooden skewer

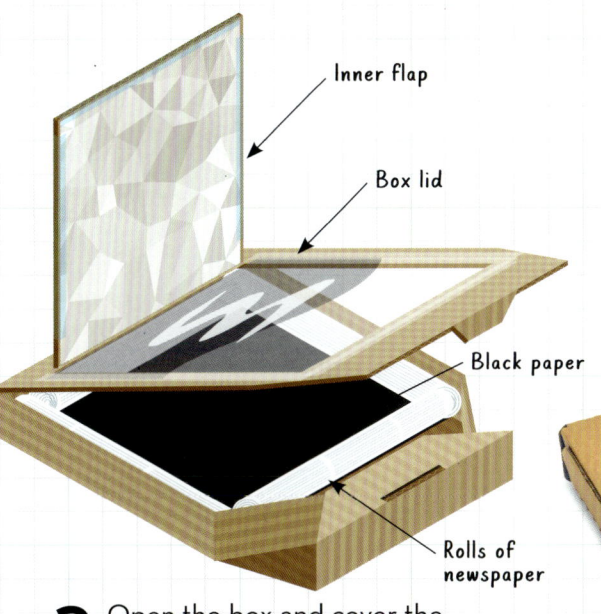

Inner flap
Box lid
Black paper
Rolls of newspaper

4 Place your food to be warmed inside the oven on the black paper. Close the lid and prop the flap open with the skewer. Place your solar oven in direct sunlight to heat it up.

Tape a metal or wooden skewer to the box lid to hold the inner lid up at an angle

3 Open the box and cover the opening in the lid with a double layer of plastic wrap, again pulled tightly across. Tape it in place. Cover the bottom with black paper, taped in place. Roll up newspaper and place it around the outside of the black paper. This will provide extra insulation.

CURIOUS CURIOSITY
Concentrated solar power (CSP) plants use mirrors to reflect sunlight onto a small area. This energy is used to make steam to drive turbines. CSP works best in places with lots of sunshine and there are plans to cover large areas of the Sahara Desert with mirrors to generate electricity.

What's the SCIENCE?
The light from the sun is reflected into the solar oven by the foil. The black paper absorbs the heat, warming the air trapped inside the plastic wrap. On a sunny day, it may reach 90°C (195°F) inside the oven – hot enough to heat up a pizza!

SOLAR POWER

44 SOLAR BUZZY BUG

Transform everyday toothbrushes into a jumping bug by using the power of the sun – and a handy spinning motor!

WHAT YOU NEED

From the kit:
- Solar panel and motor

From your home:
- 3 toothbrushes
- Toothpick
- Tape
- Modelling clay

⚠️ **1** Ask an adult to cut off the heads of the toothbrushes. Tape them together side by side.

2 Break the toothpick in half and tape each half across the toothbrushes, as shown. This is your bug's body.

Toothpick halves taped to top of the toothbrushes

3 Tape the motor to one end of the body with the spindle pointing out, as shown. Tape the solar panel behind the motor.

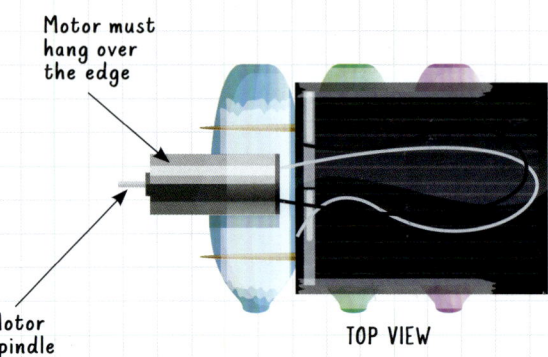

Motor must hang over the edge

Motor spindle

TOP VIEW

CURIOUS CURIOSITY

Plants and trees capture the energy of the sun in a process called photosynthesis, which takes place in their leaves. Photosynthesis uses a gas in the air called carbon dioxide and releases the gas oxygen. This is great for us, as we need oxygen when we breathe in and we breathe out carbon dioxide as a waste product.

4 Shape a small piece of modelling clay into a sausage and attach it to the spindle at one end, so that its weight is unevenly spread. Place your bug in sunlight and watch it scuttle along!

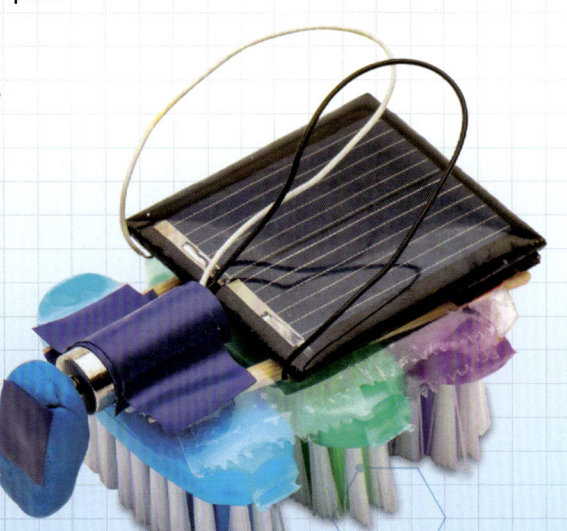

What's the SCIENCE?

The motor makes the bug vibrate. These vibrations are transferred to the bristles of the toothbrushes, moving the bug around.

SOLAR POWER

COOLING FAN 45

Keep your cool when out in the sun with this solar-powered fan.

WHAT YOU NEED
From the kit:
- Solar panel and motor

From your home:
- Small foam sheet block
- Wooden block
- Tape
- Propeller template (see page 56)

1 Tape the foam sheet block to the wooden block. Tape the solar panel motor to the top of the block. Take the propeller head (made as on page 56) and attach it to the motor. Put your fan in a brightly lit place to start the blades spinning.

BACK VIEW

What's the SCIENCE?
As the blades spin around they push air forward to produce a cooling breeze of air.

46 NIGHT LIGHT

Can't find your way in the dark? Then light your path to bed with this solar-powered night light.

WHAT YOU NEED
From your home:
- Mason jar
- Solar path light (available from garden stores)
- Piece of card big enough to cover the top of the jar
- Tape • Scissors

1 Twist off the top of the solar path light. Cut out a piece of card the size of the top of the jar and cut out a window the size of the path light's solar panel. Tape the path light to the card and fix it to the top of the jar with the solar panel pointing up.

2 Charge the panel in sunlight for a few hours. Your night light will light up when it gets dark.

What's the SCIENCE?
Solar cells at the top of the solar path lights charge a battery when placed in daylight. A sensor detects darkness and turns on the light, powered by the battery.

... TAKE IT FURTHER!
Create different lighting effects by painting the sides of the jar.

SOLAR CAR

47 SOLAR CAR

Make this mini solar car from the kit and watch it zoom along with the power of the sun!

WHAT YOU NEED
From the kit:
- Solar car kit

From your home:
- Modelling clay

1 Fasten the four brackets to the board with the nuts and bolts using the mini screwdriver. Leave one hole in one of the brackets unfastened, as shown.

2 Pull the large gear wheel to one end of its axle and push this axle through the top holes of the brackets so that the gear is by the bracket with just one nut. The small rim on the gear should be on the inner side.

3 Secure the other end of the axle in place with a washer. Push the front axle through the brackets at the front and secure with two washers.

4 Push the wheels into the four ends of the axles so that they are securely in place and turn the car over.

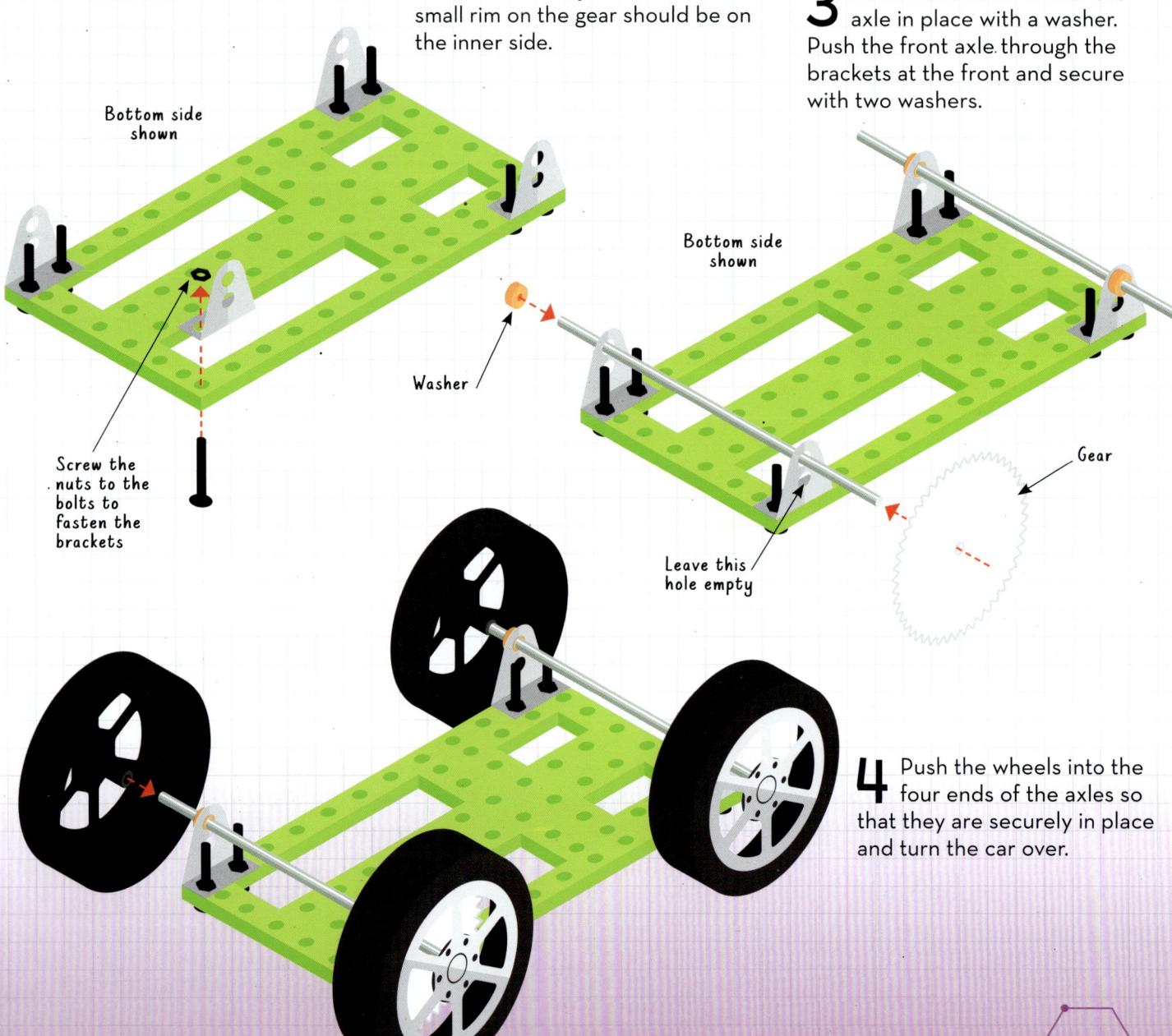

SOLAR CAR

What's the SCIENCE?

The gear on the motor interlocks with the gear on the rear wheel. There are eight teeth on the small gear and 48 teeth on the large gear. This means that six rotations of the motor's spindle drive one rotation of the car's wheels.

5 Secure the motor to the board over the large gear using the bracket. The bolts should go through the second-last hole from the end and the fourth-last hole, as shown. The teeth of the small gear wheel on the motor should interlock with the large gear wheel.

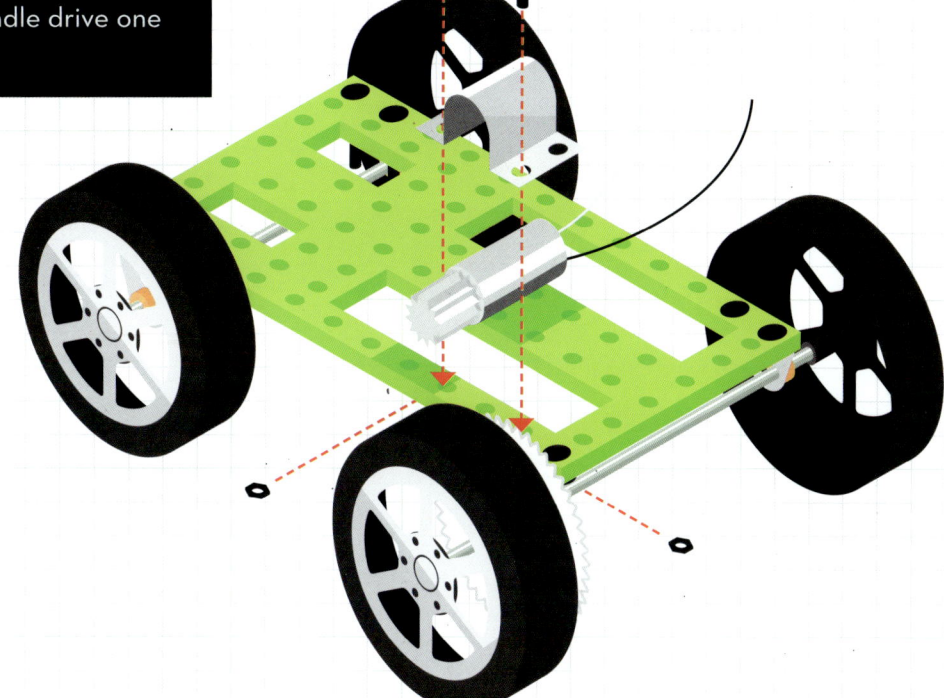

Secure the bracket with nuts and bolts

CURIOUS CURIOSITY

Every two years, a race is held to cross Australia in a solar-powered car. The course, from Darwin to Adelaide, is 3,022 km (1,878 miles) long. It takes the cars between four and seven days to complete the course, driving during the day and resting at night.

6 Place your solar race car in the sun and watch it go!

NOTES